START HERE

. . . .

"The story about Jesus is a simple one; so is His message. This is a book that blows the foam off the top and gives His simple message uncomplicated, accurate freshness. Whether you are thinking about a friendship with Jesus, started one recently, or know it's been years in the making, you're going to enjoy this book and the clarity of the message. It's all about what love does when it comes to earth and what happens next."

Bob Goff, author of *New York Times* bestseller *Love Does*

"Start Here is kind of like a Get to Know God 101 course—with clear, easy-to-understand answers to all your basic questions about what it means to be a Christian. What a relief! I can think of five people I want to give this book to."

Elisa Morgan, speaker and author of *The Beauty of Broken*

"*Start Here* introduces basic Christianity to serious enquirers (and to Christians!) in multiple personal ways and was written by two authors who clearly love Jesus Christ and who want their readers to share that love within the church universal and out in a needy world. I warmly recommend it."

F. Dale Bruner, author of commentaries on the gospels of Matthew and John and the Holy Spirit in the book of Acts

"This book is primer for those who have experienced a stirring in their soul and are looking for the path to a full relationship with Jesus. On the very first pages, David Dwight and Nicole Unice acknowledge these stirrings and then offer practical steps about what do next. If you feel that peculiar spiritual itch, that slight discomfort in your heart, that nagging irritation that cannot be soothed except through the balm of Jesus, then *Start Here* is the place to begin."

Frank A. James III, DPhil, PhD, president and professor of historical theology at Biblical Seminary

"As a church leader, I'm always on the look out for resources to recommend to people who are beginning a journey of faith. David and Nicole have done a brilliant job of simplifying concepts of faith while showcasing the beauty of starting a relationship with Jesus. Every church leader would benefit from adding *Start Here* to their discipleship process."

Jenni Catron, executive director of Cross Point Church and author of *Clout*

"If you're coming alive through new faith in Jesus Christ, I hope you'll get your hands on this book! And if you're a person who's helping others find Jesus, you'll be very glad to have this resource to share. I'm thrilled David and Nicole have written this book, which fills a huge need and helps all of us be reminded again about what Christ has done for us!"

Norm Miller, chairman of Interstate Batteries and cofounder of I AM SECOND

"All congregations need a resource that can help new believers grow into what God has called them to be. *Start Here* can be just such a resource. I see it being very helpful in new members classes, in discipleship for new believers, and even as a kind of primer for believers who need a stimulus to grow."

Jim Singleton, associate professor of pastoral leadership and evangelism at Gordon-Conwell Theological Seminary

"Have you felt yourself strangely drawn to the person of Jesus Christ, even without knowing much about Him? Have you found yourself in a relationship with Jesus, wanting to know more about what it's all about and where it all goes from here? It's hard to imagine more capable guides into what relationship with Jesus is like than David Dwight and Nicole Unice, authors of *Start Here*. They've watched carefully as others have walked this way. They don't assume they know everything about you. But I bet you'll recognize the experience of coming into the relationship that they describe. In fresh language that's never preachy, always kind, and consistently committed to what's real, Dwight and Unice take up a conversation with people like us: attracted to Jesus, confused by some of what we've heard about Him, reluctant about religion, open to checking our impressions against the facts. I can't think of a better place to start this journey into the most important relationship you'll ever have than ... well ... *Start Here*."

Dr. David A. Baer, president and
CEO of Overseas Council

"Practical, loving, gracious, and highly approachable. David and Nicole made great choices in focusing on the key elements of Christianity in *Start Here*, and they managed to tackle deep theology without using insider church language that many new believers find off-putting. The use of actual stories of those new to their journey of faith, the practical nature of the material, and the tone of the book, which is filled with humor and generosity, made me excited to see how God will use this material in the lives of those who are starting their journeys with Christ. I have been a believer for almost forty years and a pastor for six, and as I read, I found myself encouraged and affirmed in my faith."

Jennifer Lefforge, lead team/pastor of
Worship Experience at Irving Bible Church

"Dwight and Unice don't just point out the starting blocks of the faith journey; they lace up their shoes and run with you for a few laps. Reminding us that it's about relationship over rules, and story over saccharine spiritual sentimentality, *Start Here* will set you on a course for the adventure of following Jesus. They will answer some important questions, but more importantly, they will help you ask the right questions. Start now with Start Here."

Heather Zempel, discipleship pastor
at National Community Church
and author of *Community Is Messy*
and *Amazed and Confused*

"*Start Here* is a great resource for those wondering where exactly to begin a journey with Jesus. It is a warm, easygoing approach to the rich life of faith that we all hope to live. With candor and a winsome spirit, Nicole and David bring people to a place of comfort and of knowing where exactly to start. A great resource for churches, small groups, and individuals."

Reverend Tracey Bianchi, pastor for
Worship and Women at Christ Church
of Oak Brook, author, and speaker

"*Start Here* is a great primer to the Christian faith. Nicole Unice and David Dwight don't 'dumb down' Christianity by any stretch—instead they offer the very basics to the Christ-curious while inviting them to enter the mysteries of our faith."

Caryn Rivadeneira, author of
Broke and *Known and Loved*

"*Start Here* is a helpful guide to beginning a relationship with Jesus Christ. The authors take pains to present the invitation of Jesus in clear, accessible, and compelling ways. Recommended for all who wonder what Christians mean when they talk about inviting Jesus into their lives."

Mike Erre, senior pastor of EvFree
Fullerton and author of *Astonished*

"A superb introduction to the Christian life written in an engaging style that will keep the interest of contemporary readers, even those with little previous knowledge of Christian truth."

Ajith Fernando, teaching
director of Youth for Christ

"This book will be *very* useful in encouraging people in our postdenominational culture. It is the engaging tool for which we have been searching that meets this generation 'where it is' without compromising the core content of the Gospel. Our large church will certainly use it to help people discover and develop a relationship with Jesus Christ."

Rufus Smith, senior pastor of Hope Presbyterian Church and former chaplain to the Houston Rockets

START **HERE**

BEGINNING

A RELATIONSHIP WITH

JESUS

DAVID DWIGHT | NICOLE UNICE

David C Cook

transforming lives together

START HERE
Published by David C Cook
4050 Lee Vance View
Colorado Springs, CO 80918 U.S.A.

David C Cook Distribution Canada
55 Woodslee Avenue, Paris, Ontario, Canada N3L 3E5

David C Cook U.K., Kingsway Communications
Eastbourne, East Sussex BN23 6NT, England

The graphic circle C logo is a registered trademark of David C Cook.

The website addresses recommended throughout this book are
offered as a resource to you. These websites are not intended
in any way to be or imply an endorsement on the part of
David C Cook, nor do we vouch for their content.

LCCN 2014931578
ISBN 978-1-4347-0731-4
eISBN 978-0-7814-1130-1

© 2014 David Dwight, Nicole Unice
The authors are represented by MacGregor
Literary Inc. of Hillsboro, OR.

The Team: Don Pape, John Blase, Amy Konyndyk,
Nick Lee, Caitlyn Carlson, Karen Athen
Cover Design: AJ Roberts

Printed in the United States of America
First Edition 2014

1 2 3 4 5 6 7 8 9 10

CONTENTS

. . . .

Introduction

GOD STIRRINGS

. . . .

We wrote *Start Here* because we wanted to help people who are seeking God or who are new in a relationship with Him. If that's you, we're thrilled for you. Now the real adventure, the real joy, the endless discovery of our infinite God begins. Either you've begun a relationship with God or you're interested in knowing more about the God who made you and who loves you beyond your wildest dreams. Either way, be sure to be honest with God. A quality search has to be authentic—no games, no facades. A real faith is an honest faith, and with God, real growth requires authentic honesty.

Regardless of where you are exactly, we suspect you may have many more questions after reading this book. We like that. You don't "do" or "master" Christianity—because you don't "do" or "master" God.

This is not like a race you finish; it's a relationship you enter. And that's the beauty of a life with God. This is where you're starting, and you have so many places to go next! An important Bible verse we want to share with you at the outset is Jeremiah 29:13: "You will seek me and find me when you seek me with all your heart."[1] That's an all-in agreement—God offers all of Himself, and we offer all of ourselves. To seek with all of your heart means to embark on an earnest journey into all of yourself—every part, in every condition. Giving Him access and authority over all of your heart is how you can experience the real God, the One who stirred your heart in the first place. When God starts to move in your life, you'll never be the same. But how He does that—well, that's as unique as each one of us.

Most people we know feel unsure of what to say when they begin to wonder about these things. They might say, "I don't really know," and, "This is weird." Maybe you are already saying or feeling these things, already wondering why you are even reading

....

1   Throughout *Start Here* there are numerous Bible references. A
        Bible reference indicates first the book of the Bible, then the
        chapter number followed by a colon, then the verse numbers. For
        example, John 3:16–17 is referring to the book of John, chapter
        3, verses 16–17.

this introduction to a book about God! We understand that—we've been there. We know what it's like to begin to wonder, to seek something more. If you have read this far, we'd guess you are the same. You've found yourself thinking about God, perhaps even arguing with yourself about all of it. You've started to ask questions, maybe only in your head, but the questions keep coming. You're wondering about this "way" that some of your friends live, wondering about how others treat all this God stuff. Even if you've been around religion or church for a while, you've realized the faith of your childhood or your Sunday morning churchgoing habit seems inadequate to support your current questions. And you are longing for more.

We've experienced it ourselves, and we've talked to many people about it too. Every person's story is different, but each person experiences this element of discomfort, or change, or "stirring": a God stirring.

God stirrings often start with saying yes to the smallest possibility of God. Maybe you've finally said yes to a friend's invitation to church. Maybe you've started to verbalize those questions you have—the big questions like what life is all about and why you are here. Some people tell us it's a culmination of things, one domino after the other, a series of events that seem beyond coincidence, finally enough to get them to at least consider a God who's real and interested in them. *God?* Seems crazy … but they are just crazy or curious enough to keep looking.

Perhaps for you, life has become hard. Your life isn't working anymore. You need to do something different because Plan A, your plan, isn't working out and you don't know where to go next. You feel confused and exhausted by doing life your own way. Perhaps you've been calling out to God, "I need help!" and you are ready to know Him and to feel Him in your life.

For others still, the stirrings are even more sur-prising: "I was just living my life, things were fine, but then …" Part of the beauty of these beginnings is the seemingly infinite creativity of God. He knows your life, your personality, your heart, and your mind. In short, He knows you better than you know yourself. So He moves in ways that speak to you. Personal ways, unique ways, like a handwritten invitation crafted and designed to get your attention.

As we begin this journey together, we (David and Nicole) want you to know that we've experienced God in this way. Looking back, we see that these begin-nings with God are important—the most important thing that's happened in our lives. Stirrings like this get your attention and speak to an inner place. They might catch you a little off guard. This stirring you are experiencing, regardless of how subtle or small it feels now, is the beginning of a new story for you, just like it was for each of us.

DAVID'S STORY

My journey began because I had a lot of questions about life—philosophical questions about why we are here and what it's all about. I began to ask religious questions, but early on I decided that since there are so many different religions, nobody really had the answers. It seemed to me that all religions were just different ways people tried to address their big questions and, moreover, their big fears. Most of the "religious people" I had met in my life were not my kind of people, which didn't help. In truth, the people I knew who were overtly religious turned me off.

But then one day in college, a friend asked me if I had ever read the Bible. Thinking of myself as an open-minded person, I said, "No, but I'd consider it." I didn't know the first thing about the Bible. I had heard of the Bible, but that was it. I didn't know there was an Old Testament and a New Testament, books, chapters, or verses. I had no idea about any of it. So I asked, "Do I just start in the beginning—like at page one?" This friend helped me understand that the Bible wasn't quite like that, and he suggested I start my journey by reading the gospel of John in the New Testament. Problem was, I didn't have a Bible. Not even a dusty one on a shelf that I'd put there to earn good-guy points. So he lent me one, and I began to read the gospel of John. His advice turned out to be good because that's when the real stirrings began for me.

I remember sitting at my desk in my college dorm room, reading the book of John. I just read. The Bible I was reading had Jesus's words in red print, and as I kept reading, it's as if those red words would lift right off the page. Weird? I think so. But true.

Looking back on that time, I'd probably sum it up like this: "I started reading John because I was an 'open-minded guy,' but then the words of Jesus started really affecting me …" This was a beginning. Small and subtle in some ways, but now I can see that it changed my entire life.

NICOLE'S STORY

My God experiences started early, winding through my childhood years and into adulthood. As I've now spent years working in student ministry, I recognize that many people have a "seed plant" experience, a time early in their lives where they recollect warm feelings about God or Jesus. My story also starts with a "seed plant."

I grew up in the church and remember being very fond of the idea of heaven starting at age five. By the time I finished high school, I thought I knew everything there was to know about God, about Jesus, and about heaven. But then … life happened. And when my life and my "firm" beliefs collided, I became discouraged and anxious. I was trying so hard to control everything in my life, and I realized controlling life wasn't possible—and it scared me. My Sunday school faith didn't have room for this kind of panic, so I was left feeling empty-handed and alone.

By my sophomore year in college, I had to admit that I didn't know everything there was to know—and that perhaps I had a truckload of facts with a thimbleful of true conviction. This ended up being very good news, although at the time I felt confused, empty, and weary. So this God stirring was a deep need in my life for significance, for healing, and for hope beyond the glittery offerings of this world. God brought me to a place where I didn't just need information about Him—I really *needed* Him. And so this was my starting place—a place where I began to discover the truth of this life, the truth of myself, and God's plan to make it all work out. I'd describe this time as "I thought I had this whole God thing figured out, but then life made me believe otherwise ..." This was my beginning. And it changed everything.

YOUR STORY

You may not think your story is inspiring or amazing—but like our stories, it's unique because it's yours. Right now, your story may be more about questions or objections to Christianity than anything else. If that's true for you, you are not alone—we understand and appreciate that. A relationship with God isn't a simplistic formula; it's an honest journey.

Your story is unique because it is God's way of showing you that He is both universal and personal. You are stirred. He is creating moments for you. This is your handcrafted invitation to a new start. But like any invitation, you can accept or decline. We would love for this book to help you accept His invitation. Reading *Start Here* is a small commitment, a chance to explore these ideas in an honest conversation at your own pace. That's how we think of this book—as a conversation. To be fair to the conversation, you should know something we already believe with all of our hearts: God is real, and He is doing something in you, which is why you've got your hands on this book! We believe the promise from Jeremiah 29:13: "You will seek me and find me when you seek me with all your heart." So that's the best starting place: a promise from Him that He wants you to find Him.

We've started with our stories, and at the beginning of each chapter we've included a story from someone who wants to share with you. These are real people using their real names and their own words. We didn't change or edit anything about their lives or how they've told their stories. They wanted to offer their experiences in the hope that you will be encouraged, and we've included these different stories because we believe that the truth is best told through a variety of voices. We hope you find them as inspiring as we do.

So yes, it's happening. You are starting a journey, and if you accept this invitation to take that first step, this journey will change your life. It will redefine you and your understanding of the world. It will reorient your priorities. It will realign your perspective. You are taking a risk—creating an opportunity for these stirrings in you to expand into knowing God's realness, His closeness, and His love. We are so glad to take these steps with you. Here we go!

Chapter 1

IT STARTS WITH JESUS

. . . .

Pete Woods, information technology manager, age forty-two

I grew up in a family of church CEOs. CEO stood for Christmas and Easter Only. My belief at the time was that there probably was a God, but He wasn't important. I never liked going to church. You had to dress up, sing a bunch of boring songs, and then listen to someone talk about passages from the Bible—a book I knew nothing about.

Then my sister became a Christian through a ministry called Young Life when she was in high school. When I came home from college, I noticed some odd things about her. She was reading the Bible and going to church on nonholidays.

I couldn't understand this. Why would anyone want to read the Bible and go to church?

Fast-forward a few years to when I started playing ultimate Frisbee with a group of people. They would invite me to go out to dinner after playing, and I became friends with many of them. I soon discovered that these people were like my sister—they also had this desire to go to church and to read the Bible.

My friends would sometimes talk about the Bible or people in the Bible. Since I did not know much about the Bible or any of its stories, I was usually very quiet during these conversations. "Luke is my favorite book in the Bible," I remember one person saying. *I didn't even know there was a book called Luke in the Bible*, I thought to myself.

After observing my sister and my friends, I decided that I should go and find out what was up with this God thing. In a way I was also looking for CliffNotes to the Bible so I would have some general understanding of what my friends were talking about. Someone at work told me about Hope Church. Hope was small at the time, and I didn't know anyone who went there. I thought it would be a safe place to go, because if I went to church with friends but didn't want to keep going, then I would have to answer questions about why I didn't want to go anymore.

After a few weeks of attending Hope, I had lunch with David, the pastor. At lunch, David and I talked about my church life growing up, why I decided to start coming to Hope, and some questions that I had about God. After lunch David gave me a Bible and suggested that I read the gospel of John. That is when my stirrings really started blossoming.

I read John in October of 1999. That is when I started to believe, and I wanted to know more about God. I didn't ask Him to come into my life then because I really didn't know I was supposed to do that. I certainly would have if I had known.

After reading John, I had to find out more about Jesus. David encouraged me to read the rest of the Gospels. I also joined a small group and started attending an adult Bible class. The people I met helped me with my doubts and increased my faith.

However, I felt behind, especially when people would talk about biblical figures like

Abraham, Paul, Job, and David. I had heard these names (with the exception of Job), but I could not tell you anything about them. I didn't even know if they were part of the Old or New Testament. I was a slow reader, and I knew that it would take me a long time to get through the entire Bible.

I talked with someone in children's ministry, and she mentioned that the children learn a different Bible story each week. I asked David if I could help out in the children's ministry so I could learn along with the kids.

I was partnered with two other men who were the small-group teachers. The kids thought that I was a teacher as well. However, most of them knew more about the Bible than I did. I enjoyed spending time with the kids, and it was a way to help me learn those Bible stories that I had never heard as a child.

Throughout my journey with God, my relationship has had its ups and downs.

However, through it all, Jesus became the most important person in my life.

If you do a quick search for a definition of Christianity, you are likely to find something about "following the teachings of Jesus." And that's true—Christianity is about following Jesus's teachings. The problem is most people turn the idea of "following Jesus" into "following rules"—and that's not the point. The story of the Bible makes it clear that the point of knowing Jesus is for a relationship, not rules. As you begin to explore what God tells us about Himself through the Bible, you are going to find that being in a loving, committed relationship with Him is the main thing. So saying that the main idea of Christianity is to follow teaching points is like saying that the main idea of marriage is to share your household bills. Not exactly what we hope for in a great love story!

RULES VERSUS RELATIONSHIP

This perspective of rules versus relationship is a great divide that distinguishes Christianity from other religions. Where most religions teach that the way to "be good" is through required practices and rigid beliefs, Christianity starts from a different place.

From the earliest times, Jesus's followers weren't known for following rules or "being good." The thing that stuck out—the thing that was worth mentioning—was the mere reality that they had "been with Jesus" (Acts 4:13). Not that they acknowledged Jesus, not that they followed the behavioral system of Jesus, but that they were "with" Him. Being with Jesus is what transformed these people from what the Bible calls "unschooled, ordinary men" into courageous, bold leaders. And that's the same reality we are offered when Jesus invites us into a relationship: to "be with Him."

IT'S ALL ABOUT RELATIONSHIP

In a good relationship, we're trying to stay in touch with each other, trying to keep close. This means we're seeking to share our thoughts and experiences because in close relationships, we share our whole lives. This is true of a relationship with God. If you read the Bible, you'll find this theme throughout—that God is love (1 John 4:8) and that He created human beings to live in full, life-giving relationship with Him.

However, it seems whether it's with other people or with God, we have ways of fouling up our relationships—by retreating into ourselves, behaving selfishly, hurting others. When this happens, we feel it. We know something is not right, and the relationship becomes distant. Over time, it can feel like there isn't a relationship at all.

But if the relationship is important, we might seek to reconcile. One of the ways we do this is by asking good questions of each other, questions like, "How are you really doing?" and, "Can you help me understand?" Such questions have the goal of bringing two people closer together, closer to a shared perspective and understanding. People who are gifted in the art of relationships are often people who ask some of the best questions. Here's where God is a pro.

THE FIRST QUESTION

Right at the beginning of the Bible, God demonstrated this aspect of His character through His relationship with Adam and Eve—a trusting, transparent, daily relationship. The example of their relationship suggests that when it comes to life with God, we've got nothing to hide and nothing to fear. In the third chapter of Genesis (the first book of the Bible), we read about Adam and Eve choosing to turn from God and live life apart from Him. When this happens, the relationship with God was broken—as happens in any close relationship when one party turns away. And when the relationship was broken, God came looking for Adam and Eve. He didn't come to punish or shame them. He came looking to restore the relationship.

The account suggests that God was saddened and hurt that the transparent relationship they had known no longer felt the same way:

> Then the man and his wife heard the sound of the LORD God as he was walking in the garden in the cool of the day, and they hid from the LORD God among the trees of the garden. But the LORD God called to the man, *"Where are you?"* (Genesis 3:8–9)

Think for a moment about the depth of this question: *Where are you?* It's essentially a directional question with the intent to find someone, and in this instance, God wanted to find Adam and Eve for the purpose of reconciling. It's the first time we see God taking an initial step to help restore the relationship that we people have broken. Since that time, He's always been taking the first steps to restore this relationship. And when you can sense God stirring in your life, you, too, are a person He's seeking out, so that you might be able to know Him and live in a relationship with Him.

Where are you? may be a geographically related question—as in, "I'm home; where are you?" But *where are you?* can be deeper, too. It can be a question about your emotional state, your thoughts or feelings. It's significant that this profoundly relational question is the first question God asks in the Bible. God is asking it because He wishes for the relationship to be restored and reconciled. It's God's first question, and it reveals His heart—that He deeply misses this relationship. If God were to ask you right now, *"Where are you?"* what might you say to Him?

ANOTHER QUESTION: *"WHAT DO YOU WANT?"*

The gospel of John in the New Testament has many parallels to the book of Genesis in the Old Testament. In the first chapter of John we see Jesus asking some curious men a question like God's question. This question was similarly profound and simple. He asked them, "What do you want?" (John 1:38). It's a pretty big question when you think about it—especially when God is the one doing the asking.

What is it that I really want from God? Do I want answers; do I want peace; do I want Him to give me hope, give me money, give me a spouse?

Perhaps surprised by the question, the men avoided it as we often do and then changed the subject. They asked Jesus, "Where are you staying?" Rather than give them an actual address, He answered them, "Come … and see" (John 1:39). This response is indicative of Jesus's invitation to a relationship with Him. Rather than giving an answer, He gives an invitation. Rather than offering an address, He offers a relationship. Rather than telling us rules, He invites us to be with Him.

Some of us might answer Jesus's question "What do you want?" with something like this: "I'm just looking for some answers" or, "I just want God to make my life better." This is understandable. If we are honest, many of us will agree that we're usually saying to God, "I want something from You," while God is saying to us, "I want to be with you." That's a very different request! We're asking God to give us something; He's asking us to be with Him. Yes, in all instances, Jesus is going to invite you to *be with* Him. "Come and see" implies being together, and that relationship will be central to the discovery.

COME AND SEE

When Jesus told these men to "come and see," He was offering them the chance to come be with Him.

He offers us the same thing: the opportunity to come check Him out. It's the first step toward a relationship. Jesus doesn't ever tell people who are truly seeking Him to go away and come back when they get their act together or jump through this hoop or that. He just invites them to follow Him. We can imagine Him saying, "Well, come along, and then we can take it from there." Relationship, not rules. A relationship with Jesus Christ. So regardless of what you've experienced with Christianity in your life, whether in church or on TV or through a billboard, the Bible tells us that the question of Christian faith—the core of faith—always starts with Jesus.

The question "who is Jesus?" is the main point of the New Testament. It's *the* question. Since Jesus is God in the flesh,[1] not just a famous religious guy, this changes everything. If He's just a religious guy, a good moral teacher, then we can learn some life lessons from Him, but that's about it. Put a little *Do unto others as you would have them do unto you* poem on our mirror, wear a cross around our neck, and be done with it. But Jesus lived a unique life and died a sacrificial death—a

....

1   In the beginning of the gospel of John, Jesus is called "the Word." Later, it says, "The Word was God." In John 1:14, it says, "The Word became flesh and made his dwelling among us."

little extreme if your goal is to be a "good teacher." C. S. Lewis said, "A man who was merely a man and said the sort of things Jesus said would not be a great moral teacher. He would be either a lunatic—on a level with the man who says he is a poached egg—or else the Devil of Hell."[2] Whew, that gives us something to think about. So who *is* Jesus?

THE NEXT QUESTION

Consider the following conversation Jesus had with His closest group of followers (called disciples):

> When Jesus came to the region of Caesarea Philippi, he asked his disciples, "Who do people say the Son of Man is?"
>
> They replied, "Some say John the Baptist; others say Elijah; and still others, Jeremiah or one of the prophets."
>
> "But what about you?" he asked. *"Who do you say I am?"* (Matthew 16:13–15)

....
2   C. S. Lewis, *Mere Christianity* (New York: HarperOne, 1952), 52.

Jesus brings the question of who He is away from a theoretical and abstract idea to a personal place. It's clear it's the question of the Bible—and remarkably, it's Jesus's question to each of us:

"Who do you say I am?"

This is where Christianity begins. Your answer to that question *is* your start here, because it's where you get clear about what you think of Jesus. Ultimately, when it comes to your life, it doesn't really matter what someone else says or thinks about Jesus—it matters what you think.

When Jesus asked His disciples this question, He didn't do it to quiz them or make them feel dumb. He asked because He wanted them to have life as all of us are intended to have it and to experience the kind of hope that only He can give. He wants us to know life in a beautiful relationship with God. He asks this question of us because He loves us and because He knows that our answer is the starting point of finding that kind of life.

So what would it feel like to have Jesus standing in front of you, asking this question? Really, imagine it. Imagine this powerful, mysterious man looking right into your eyes, asking you this question. We imagine we'd be a little hesitant to answer. It would be one of those moments that feel important, where we'd want to have the right thing to say. Maybe if we were quick on our feet, we'd answer with another question:

"Jesus, You're not really an easy person to figure out. You do remarkable things, but in other ways You seem pretty much like us. So I wonder, who do *You* say You are?"

JESUS RE: JESUS

Fortunately, what Jesus says about Himself is recorded in the Bible. The words He used are sometimes referred to as the "I AM" statements of Jesus, and they include the following:

> "I am God's Son." (John 10:36)
> "I am the light of the world." (John 8:12)
> "I am the resurrection and the life." (John 11:25)
> "I am the way and the truth and the life." (John 14:6)
> "I am the good shepherd." (John 10:11)

"I am!" (John 8:58)

With this last statement, Jesus also made an audacious claim about Himself: that He doesn't just know about God or teach about God, but that He *is* God.[3] These are just some of Jesus's statements, the way He would answer the question about His identity. But Jesus doesn't stop; He makes it even more personal.

THE BIG QUESTION: *"DO YOU BELIEVE THIS?"*

In another story in the Bible, Jesus was talking with a friend of His named Martha. Jesus had just told her an incredible thing, a thing that ordinary people wouldn't say: "I am the resurrection and the life" (John 11:25). He then went on to say,

> "The one who believes in me will live, even though they die; and whoever lives by believing in me will never die. *Do you believe this?*" (John 11:25–26)

---

3   Jesus clarified His equality with God when He said, "Before Abraham was born, I am!" (John 8:58). This refers directly to the Old Testament, when God described Himself: "I AM WHO I AM" (Exodus 3:14).

Jesus always makes things personal. He said to His disciples, "But what about you—who do *you* say I am?" and He said to Martha, "Do *you* believe this?" Jesus asks these same questions to us, too, and answering these questions is a part of being in a relationship with God, of finding God and finding the truth. And finding the truth starts with Jesus Christ. Jesus Christ—the living, breathing man who walked on this earth thousands of years ago. Jesus Christ—the man who millions of people have built their lives around for thousands of years. It all starts here. God stirs us, and the stirring brings us to Jesus. And that's what happened with Josh.

JOSH'S STORY

Josh represents everything we love about young people. He's passionate about what he believes, he's earnest, and he's honest. While we were driving to a college conference, I (Nicole) asked Josh to tell me his story of faith, and he smiled and leaned forward as he began. Raised mostly by a single mom who managed to hold life together for him and his brother, Josh grew up in a family that didn't recognize God at all. His mom "found Jesus" when Josh was in high school, and Josh hated what she became. He refused to go to church with her and became angry about everything, and he wasn't even sure why. He expressed his anger by doing everything that would make his mom sad—running around to parties, moving from one drink to the next and one girl to the next.

Then he headed off to college, glad to be away from it all. But at school something happened. He became friends with a bunch of guys—and it turns out they were all Christians. One night, he had a powerful spiritual experience. He describes it this way: "It was like Jesus came to me and slapped me in the face with a two-by-four."

Now, let me interrupt Josh's story and tell you that I've never felt like Jesus slapped me with a two-by-four, and my guess is Josh's mom hasn't experienced that either. But the amazing thing about God is that He comes to each of us in a way that is unique, a way that is powerful and just what we need. And as Josh tells the story, the two-by-four was exactly what he needed. He recalls that evening as a personal wake-up call from Jesus to him about his way of living and about what he was missing. It was the moment that started his honest journey, when he began to seek out the question of "who is Jesus?"

Maybe you've experienced a stirring or felt a longing in your heart for more than the life you're living.

Maybe you've had a more dramatic experience—one where you feel your heart moving within you—and maybe, like Josh, you've had a two-by-four moment. But whatever has brought you here, it's your answer to this question—*who is Jesus?*—that really matters. And just remember, it's not our answer or Josh's answer—it's yours. Who do *you* say Jesus is?

Jesus asked His disciples and He asks each of us,

What do you want?

Who do you say I am?

Do you believe this?

No matter where you are with those questions, His invitation is the same:

Come and see.

Chapter 2

OBSTACLES

. . . .

**Paige Butcher, middle school
teacher, age twenty-five**

I knew and accepted God as a child but later
drifted away. But after I separated myself from
church and from God, there was definitely a season of Him stirring and working to draw me back
toward Him. At the time, I was in college, and I
was going through a season of feeling hugely dis-
illusioned about Christianity. All of it felt tinny and
false to me, and I began to wonder about everything, right down to God's existence. At that time,
a friend of mine bought me a documentary about
my favorite Christian songwriter, Sara Groves.
Somehow I still liked Sara; she was authentic and
real to me, so I respected her music.

I remember lying in my bed in my student apartment and crying through that entire DVD. In the film, Sara and her husband pack up their tour bus and drive down to Louisiana right after Hurricane Katrina. They didn't know where they were headed or what they would find, but they had the resources, so they just went. I realized that night that in the midst of my emotional turmoil and spiritual confusion, I had all but lost faith in humanity and God's ability to redeem it. I realized the real Jesus Christ is different from the stale and hostile religion that I'd encountered so frequently.

I think I was struggling with doubt. I was worried that maybe it was illogical and silly to believe there is a God. I worried that this whole religion thing was a construct designed to assuage the fears and shortcomings of the human race. There were so many things I didn't know about science and philosophy and life in general, so I worried about blindly buying into something that so many people consider to be nonsense. If they'd searched, studied, and analyzed and found it all to be impossible, then maybe it was. What could I know that they didn't?

I wrote this in a blog back in 2008: "I'm just desperately looking for answers to questions— I am not looking for anything other than the truth, and whatever that is, I'll follow it passionately and wholeheartedly."

In the midst of this time, I started a conversation with God. I think prayer came before anything. I wanted to find a way to communicate with God honestly. I figured that He knew my heart and my confusion in all of it and that He would help me sort it out. I had a very strong conviction that God would prefer my honest doubt over any kind of pious insincerity, so I decided to just lay it all out on the table before God. It felt a little weird at first because I still had some nagging doubts and wondered if maybe I was just praying to the wall, but something kept me going even so.

I also began attending church every once in a while ... and I was *very* timid and reluctant about it. I would roll my eyes, squirm uncomfortably, or stifle a gag during just about every sermon—I had such a low tolerance for any kind of "churchiness"—but I did manage to leave feeling somewhat encouraged.

I don't really know how it happens or how it all
logically works out, but the closer I get to God and
the more I find a way to be authentic with Him—to
let go of all of my needs for control and power—
I see that I really am worth something. To Him, to
the world, and I guess to myself, too. I still have my
moments of struggling, but it feels like there's been
a shift in my core, and those kinds of changes can't
be faked or brought about on our own.

I'm never going to find all the logical guaran-
tees that I might want, but somehow, through the
mystery of God, His presence is unmistakable in
my life.

Recently I (David) had a meaningful conversation
with a woman named Emily. Emily has a beautiful,
humble spirit about her, and she came to my office
to talk about some theological questions. Emily is
a follower of Christ—she's received Him and she is
seeking Him—and she still has questions. I like that
a lot. Sometimes it may seem that once you receive
Jesus, you're no longer seeking Him. However, once
we start with Him, once we enter into the exploration

of *who is Jesus?* we are usually hungry to know more. And that's why I liked my discussion with Emily.

Emily told me about a conversation she'd had with a colleague at work. They have a nice friendship, and often when the topic of faith and religion comes up, the conversation turns to Christian faith. In a recent conversation about Christianity, Emily's friend said to her, "You know *all of this* isn't true, don't you?" Wow, what a conversation starter!

And so I asked Emily what her friend meant by the phrase *all of this*. Seems that when a person says "all of this," referring to Christian belief, that phrase may include a remarkably large accumulation of thoughts, conversations, issues, and doubts around faith, the Bible, the church, and Christian people in general. I appreciate Emily's coworker because at one time in my life I would have said something similar. In response to my question, Emily told me the very real hurts and doubts her friend had about faith. Emily's coworker touches on something we all have to deal with when we begin to look for Jesus: our *all of this* pile.

ALL OF THIS

None of us comes to the questions of faith with a clean slate. We bring our stuff—our background, mixed with any religious experiences we may have, our upbringing, the dynamics of relationships with our parents and family members. We bring our doubts about the world; we bring our personal hurts.

Think of your own objections to Christianity. Maybe you've said or heard something like this: "I'm fine with Jesus; it's those church people I can't stand." Or maybe it was a question: "If God is good, why is there evil?" Or, "How can there be only one way to heaven?" We affirm these questions and believe in the importance of asking them. For most of us, these questions and many others are in our *all of this* pile—questions we may be carrying around inside of us.

Then there are the "on the outside" issues that may also be part of our *all of this* pile. The outside issues and obstacles to Christianity may include everything from politics, to social issues, to debates about the Bible, to evolution/creation discussions, to religion in schools, to church and state, to problems with the institutional church, to things we read in the news, to what our friends think and what our family thinks. If you put these things into the *all of this* pile, it's no surprise that moving toward Jesus often feels like an uphill climb.

"BUT WHAT ABOUT ... ?"

Julie pulled me (Nicole) aside during a Bible study. I didn't really know Julie, except to say that I had noticed her. Over the past several weeks I'd been teaching about encounters people in the Bible had with Jesus, and even though I was teaching a large group of people, I noticed Julie. There was something about her face as she listened to the teaching—a mix of confusion, doubt, and hope—and so I was glad when she wanted to talk. "I don't know about all this Jesus stuff," she said to me. Even as we spoke, those same expressions—confusion, doubt, and hope— flashed on her face. "I mean, it sounds good"—flash of hope—"but how could Jesus really be the only way?"—flash of confusion—"Are you trying to tell me that there are all these people in the world who have it wrong?"—flash of anger, doubt.

Most of us are like Julie. As soon as we encounter Jesus, we also encounter a whole range of emotions. And we can get skittish when we get into the "but what abouts?" If you've got questions like this going on—that's a good sign. Even if the "but what abouts?" create discomfort or ambivalence in you, that's still a good sign. God stirrings can be an uncomfortable feeling. Some of your deepest assumptions about life may be challenged. So you want to learn, you want to know more about God—which requires some thinking and can be unsettling. Remember, a big part of the journey of the Christian life is learning; that's one reason Christ followers are called *disciples*. A disciple is a student, a learner, a follower. And if God is as big as we believe He must be, then we'll be asking questions and learning throughout our whole lives with Him.

Julie immediately came up against one of the biggest "but what about" questions—the exclusivity of Jesus, the big claim that He is the only way to God. It's true; He said it: "No one comes to the Father except through me" (John 14:6).

For me (David) this was a major obstacle in my spiritual search. I know I'm not the only one. There are two roads we could take to address this. One is a deep theological road, rooted in Bible study and big questions like, "How is it that our sins are actually forgiven?" The other is a "let's get the main idea" road, and since this book is called *Start Here*, that's the one we'll take.   •

WHO'S THE CAPTAIN?

Picture this: Imagine you've hustled to the airport to catch a flight for an important business meeting.

Packed: check. Parking deck: check. Boarding pass: check. Photo ID: check. Waiting in line to go through security: ugh. The undignified experience of taking off shoes and belt, getting the computer out, putting toiletries in the ziplock bag, feeling rushed even though the people behind you are trying to be nice: check. Putting the belt back on, shoes back on, computer back in bag, watch back on, looking for a good cup of coffee: check. Drinking good coffee, spending a few quiet moments at the gate: check. Yes, a few quiet moments! Listening as zones are called (should you jump the gun and sneak in an earlier zone?), then jumping in line: check. Finding your seat, putting your bag in the right place, finally sitting, taking note that the person next to you is small (yes!): check. Made it!

At this point, the pilot comes over the speaker and says something like this (if he's in a good mood): "Good morning, everybody, this is the captain speaking from the flight deck—welcome aboard flight 343 headed for Chicago." In that moment, your brain immediately confirms that you are going to Chicago. You feel good about that—yep, you are going in the right direction. Imagine the person next to you panics when he hears the captain speaking. He immediately jumps up and tries to get off the plane before it pushes back from the gate and he flies thousands of miles in the wrong direction!

What's the point? First of all, the captain made a clear announcement about where the plane is going. When he did, it would have been unlikely that you would have thought, *Who is* he *to tell me where this plane is going? This is my seat, I paid for it, and I can go where I want.* On the contrary, the clarity that the captain gave was very helpful, and this flight is going to only one place: Chicago. Furthermore, the fact that the captain was the one who made the announcement gives confidence that it's an accurate statement. If the small guy next to you who is reading a book called *Flying for the First Time* said it, you'd be a lot less confident. Your comfort is based on your confidence in the captain. When he started the announcement, he said, "This is the captain speaking." His assurance and accurate information give confidence that he is who he says he is.

So now think about Jesus in this way: when Jesus said, "I am the way and the truth and the life" (John 14:6), the first thing we're likely to think is, *Is He really?* It's similar to the evaluation we make when we hear the static from the loudspeaker in the airplane cabin: *Is this the captain?*

"WHO'S THE CAPTAIN?!?"

One more example might be helpful. Let's say that we are vacationing on a big cruise ship. Then the unimaginable happens—the ship has an accident, and it's taking on water. Alarms sound; the ship is sinking. We are in a room several stories below the deck, and people start coming out into the hallway, frantically talking about what's happening and how to get to safety. Water begins to rise into our hallway, and a number of us find a room that seems safe and dry, at least for the moment. More water is coming down the hallway, and now people are going left and right, water rushing in on all sides. Other people start yelling, "Follow me—I know the way!" We watch some people do that, and a door is opened and more water pours in. It's getting worse, and that's definitely not the way.

Then a man comes running down the hallway in knee-deep water—and he says, "Ladies and gentlemen, I am the captain. I know this ship down to the smallest detail. I've come down to find you, and I can tell you that there is one way to safety. Follow me."

Again our minds run calculations. "Is he really the captain?" is our first question. Our answer to that has everything to do with whether we would trust him or not, follow him or not. He's dressed in white pants, the uniform of most of the crew, but he's stripped down to a plain white T-shirt. Perhaps we ask him some quick questions to try to determine if he really is the captain—or perhaps we are just relieved he's there to help. When we are convinced of his identity, our initial response is gratitude—an outpouring of "thank you so much for coming down here to get us!" And then we follow him; actually, we don't let him out of our sight. We stay very close to him, as close as possible the whole time we are seeking to get to safety.

The question in the cruise ship analogy is similar to the airplane. The important question is, "Are you the captain?" But when we imagine ourselves on the ship, we recognize that the stakes are much higher than on that airplane. Our very lives are at risk. And since a crisis is upon us, we are not likely to say, "Who are *you* to tell me that you know the only way out? I can go whichever way I choose." If those were our words, the captain might reply, "Well, okay, you're free to go whichever way you choose, but I can tell you that I know there is only one way to get to safety. But if you want to try another way, feel free."

In this instance, it's unlikely that we'd begin a debate about our right to choose our own way. Because if he's really the captain, well, then he knows the way.

THE REAL CAPTAIN

One way to describe Jesus is as a rescuer on a rescue mission. When Jesus said, "I am the way and the truth and the life," He didn't say, "I am *a* way and *a* truth and *a* life." Our question to Him is similar to our questions to the captain of the plane or the ship because we want to know, "Are You really the captain (the Son of God)?"

As life progresses, many of us gradually develop a disinterest toward this question. Most of us feel comfortable just trying to get a seat with enough legroom on the plane. And most of us aren't facing our mortality with the kind of intensity that we would be on a sinking ship. But having confidence in the captain is the main question in both analogies.

On the ship, your belief (or not) in the captain would make all the difference. Same with Jesus. If it's a rescue mission, we are less likely to say, "I can go whichever way I please." Yes, you could if you would like, but if He really is the captain, the one who knows all of the nuances of human existence, then He really does know the way. Or maybe as you start exploring what the Bible says about Jesus, you begin to ask yourself the question, "Do I believe He knows the way?"

If you're reading this book, you may or may not yet have come to the point where you have said yes to this question. Or you may have said, "Yes, I believe. But I still have questions." If that's you, we're with you and we're for you. Keep the questions coming. Good questions are how we grow. Doubts and uncertainties are not unusual. But let's say you agree that Jesus might know the way. If that's true, the first question you might have is, "What do I need to do to get going that way?" And this is where Jesus surprises us. He doesn't say, "Follow this." He says, "Follow Me." The captain of the cruise ship didn't point us to a map; he pointed us to himself. Jesus also points to Himself, and He invites us to commit.

A COMMITTED RELATIONSHIP

In most cultures the pinnacle of committed relationship is marriage. So it's interesting to note that in the New Testament, God uses the analogy of marriage to describe how He relates to us.

The way I (Nicole) began a relationship with my husband, Dave, started off like many love stories do. There was mutual interest (well, a little more on my part). That interest led to time spent together. And as we began spending time together, experiencing everyday life together, somewhere along the way we crossed over from a casual "hang-outship" to a relationship.

A relationship starts when we hear about a person and are open to getting to know him or her. This applies to friendship and to dating, and here we apply it to knowing Jesus. Knowing Jesus starts with being open to getting to know Him. Perhaps a friend invites you to church or to a Bible study. You may hesitantly give it a try. The "hesitantly" part feels surprisingly similar to saying yes to a date when you aren't sure if you like the other person!

Let's say you go to the Bible study and have a generally positive experience. You weren't freaked out, nobody made you feel weird, nobody asked you to pray out loud, and the stuff you heard about Jesus seemed real to you. If you had an experience like that, you might go home thinking, *Wow—I'm not the religious type … but that was okay.*

The day after that experience, you find yourself thinking a little bit about this Jesus. You are somewhat intrigued. Learning about Jesus seems different from "being one of those religious types." Your friend invites you back next week, and so you go. Again you have a pretty good experience. Again you find yourself thinking about Jesus. You may wonder if *all of this* is really true, if Jesus could be real and a person you can know. Later that week, a conversation with your friend turns to spiritual things. In a nonthreatening way she asks you, "What are your thoughts about what you've heard?" A meaningful conversation ensues, and the friend provides sincere listening and helpful encouragement.

It's kind of like you have had a couple of dates now, where Jesus is beginning to be real to you as you are checking Him out. Then your friend invites you to go to a cookout, saying, "Some friends from the Bible study are going to be there, along with a few other people." And, since you're in "so far so good" mode, you decide to go.

When you arrive, people seem to be having a good time, and you generally like the vibe. Then someone comes over to you and says, "So tell me how you got saved." Almost spitting up your hot dog, you manage to cough out a profound response: "What!?" Then the person says, "You know, when did you give your life to Jesus Christ?"

This person asking these questions is not helping your tentative exploration of a relationship with Jesus. Looking for a quick exit, you say, "Hey, great to see you; you know, I need to put some Coke on my hot dog," and off you go, looking for your friend so you can ask, "What the heck?!" Yeah, you just hit a rough patch.

As you're on your way home that evening, your friend says, "Don't worry too much about what John said to you. He's kind of an 'out there' person, and he's just trying to be nice."

You say, "Yeah, well, this is *my* life, and I'm not 'giving' it to a guy named Jesus who I hardly know and I think is dead."

Your friend smiles and says, "Try to know that people mean well, even if they say something that freaks you out. It doesn't mean that Jesus isn't real; it just means that that person made you cough up your hot dog. Keep seeking Jesus, and try not to worry too much about a person who trips you up. It's not about you and John. It's about you and Jesus."

As the relationship journey continues, it feels like a couple of steps forward—and now a few steps back. It would be nice if this whole Jesus thing happened in a few easy steps. But it won't because that's not what Christianity truly is—it's a relationship. And true to almost all relationships, it inevitably has some bumps, some stops and starts.

A GROWING RELATIONSHIP

Fast-forward a few months. You are finding that your interest in Jesus is a bit unpredictable. You have some encouraging experiences or learning discoveries, and then you hear or read something about the Bible and think, *You've got to be kidding me. That's crazy.* If you're like most people, the journey happens kind of like this—one way or another.

You have been attending the Bible study with your friend now for a while, and despite the bumps, something is happening. You are beginning to feel alive, more excited about life, more open to the idea that God could be real. You are thinking about things—life, challenges, relationships—on a different level. Perhaps if God is real, and if He really is good, and if He really is love, and if He really does love *you*, then this is a big deal.

You decide to begin reading the Bible on your own—and with the help of your friend, you are able to make progress with some of your questions. You're beginning to feel a sense of optimism about life that you have never felt before. You are beginning to pray simple prayers to Jesus like, "Jesus, if You're real, I want to know more of You, and if You're not, I expect no response."

Now, if you step back for a moment and consider what's happening in your life, you begin to realize that you have an acquaintance relationship with Jesus

Christ. In other words, you've heard of Him; you know a little about Him; you've met Him; you've hung out a little bit. You are in the "hang-outship" of early relationships, and there is very little commitment on your part. That's enough for now as far as you are concerned. Fair enough. This is how all relationships develop and grow, and Christianity, as we have said, is a relationship—a personal relationship with Jesus Christ.

If this was all you ever knew about Christianity—that it's about Jesus, it's about what He said, and it's about your relationship with Him—then you could appreciate how simple this is. But if you've spent any time around church or Christians, you might also think, *Then why do some Christians seem to make Christianity about rules—constantly sizing people up and measuring who's good and who's not? That kind of religion seems more like God as Santa Claus, "making a list, checking it twice—keeping track of who's naughty and nice."*

If you're thinking this, you may have a valid observation. But then you're reminded about something your friend said: "Don't get too caught up in what other people do and how they do it. Keep seeking to know Jesus." Our friend Katie[1] said it like

. . . .

1   You can read Katie's story in her own words at the beginning of chapter 5.

this: "If I could tell my old self one thing, I would say, 'All the rules you were supposed to follow don't matter—forget them and follow Jesus.'"

Chapter 3

RECEIVING JESUS

. . . .

Heather Beam, mom of five, age forty

Until my early twenties, I lived what I'd call the "average" American adolescent experience—surviving years of great peer influence coupled with a good dose of insecurity about who I was and what was valuable about me; spending as much time as possible with my friends; and experiencing my first serious, intimate relationship.

I started dating my now-husband, JD, when I was twenty-one. He was the first person I'd dated who was a Christian and who spoke openly about "the good Lord" (his words). Although he wasn't living much of a Christian lifestyle in college, he at least had a foundational faith that was very appealing to me. A couple of years into my relationship with JD, God brought a couple of friends into our lives who invited us to come to church with them. They had something—a joy, a peace, a loving way about them—that I wanted. JD and I were discussing our future, so the idea of going to church together was intriguing. We went only a handful of times, but those few experiences (doing something "good" and "right" together when all of our friends were doing just the opposite) started that growth for me. Convictions about our behavior and choices began to set in, and we started to feel less inclined toward our previous ways of doing things. Partying with friends, having sex outside of marriage, and living together all became unappealing to us. We made a decision to stop being intimate and kept that commitment to each other and to God for the year and a half leading up to our wedding.

Hands down, my greatest obstacle to embracing my newfound faith was what my friends would think of me. And it wasn't just that—JD and I struggled with the very process of change. We wanted to change; we didn't want to; we wanted to; we didn't. It was a process of letting go and asking God to transform our hearts.

Shortly after we got married, we felt compelled to find a church. Prior to getting involved in church, I had never felt a true sense of acceptance and belonging from a community of friends—ever! I never felt like I was part of the in crowd. Accepting Christ and choosing to follow Him and feeling the warmth of His love and acceptance was the first time I felt like I was in the in crowd. I know that sense of acceptance and belonging is one of our greatest yearnings in life—the first Bible verse that ever brought tears to my eyes (after seeing it on a bumper sticker!) was Jeremiah 1:5 ("Before I formed you in the womb I knew you").

It took me until I was almost thirty-five to *really* take in how much He loves me and that I do not have to perform for Him or be perfect in some way—that I can come to Him with all my flaws and failures and that He will take me in His arms and hug me and tell me He *knows*—and that He wants me for His own.

Here's a great question to ask a married couple: "What happened on your first date?" An even greater question to ask a married couple: "When did you fall in love?" Answering the first question gets you some variety while answering the second pushes you into what we call *mystery*. The mystery of love and the way that it develops between two people are what make a great story. When it comes to God, the Bible says that He is the source of all things (1 Corinthians 8:6) and that He is love (1 John 4:16). So when we think about knowing God, understanding that He is the source of love is a good starting point. Our relationship with Jesus—and how we get to that relationship—is the start of a great love story.

Since Jesus's first invitation to us is, "Follow Me," it's clear now that He's inviting us to be in a relationship. At first the relationship begins with following. In a sense, that's what happens when you date. You are not committed; you are learning; you are exploring.

But after a while, the relationship arrives at a place where a conversation is needed. This conversation seeks clarity about the nature of the relationship. This might be called the DTR conversation: "Define the Relationship." Usually this conversation has significant results because it elicits a sense of either greater commitment or lesser commitment from one or both.

When I (David) wanted to make my feelings known to my now-wife, Elisabeth, we were having lunch together. I got up the courage and asked, "Have you ever thought about our relationship being more than friends?" She was quiet for a moment and then said, "No." *Hmm*, I thought. *Bummer.*

I was determined that wouldn't be the end of the story for me, and she now says that when I sought this clarity, even though she turned me down, it got her thinking about us in a different way. If I hadn't asked that question, we might still be "just friends."

The heart of that conversation with Elisabeth was, "What are we doing, and what are your intentions?" Now put this same idea into the context of a relationship with Jesus. What if Jesus said to you, "I've really enjoyed the time we've been spending together, but I'm wondering if you see this as a committed relationship, or if you see it as just hanging out?" Many people date forever without making a commitment, and in a sense many people do this with Jesus. They like the idea of Jesus—a Jesus who listens to their prayers and gives comfort when needed and hangs around at weddings and funerals—but they don't feel a *need* or *love* for Him. They *like* Him.

This idea of liking Jesus seems fine, but as we've mentioned already, the New Testament description of Jesus's relationship with us is that of marriage (John 3:28–29; Revelation 19:7–9). Imagine if you were looking for a spouse you wanted to be with only at certain times and seasons, for your own interests and desires. Not exactly the makings of a great marriage, huh? Some men look for a trophy wife—and some of us are looking for a "trophy Jesus." A Jesus who makes us look good.

Jesus, however, is a committer, and He's offering Himself so that people might respond with a relational commitment—and as we've said previously, He doesn't start with "follow the rules," but "follow Me." Check out these examples:

- Jesus found Simon Peter and his brother Andrew fishing from their boats and said, "Follow Me." They immediately left what they were doing and began to spend the rest of their lives as disciples of Jesus (Matthew 4:18–20).

- Jesus found Levi sitting at his
  tax collector's booth and said,
  "Follow Me." Levi got up immediately and became a disciple
  (Mark 2:14).

In both cases, maybe surprisingly, the guys who
followed Jesus didn't know what they were getting into.
They had seen Jesus do some amazing stuff, but at that
point in Jesus's life, it wasn't really clear what He was all
about. The disciples didn't have books and movies and
podcasts and blog posts and a church on every corner
trying to sell Jesus to them. All they had was the person
of Jesus, some experience that got their attention, and
the invitation to follow Him. In this way, we're back to
the similarities to marriage. Many people who've been
married awhile look back to their wedding day as the
beginning of a real relationship together. This relationship starts with trusting the other person without truly
knowing him or her deeply. It can't be any other way—
you get to know each other deeply only by doing life
together. And it's the same with Jesus.

We learn from stories in the Bible that Jesus isn't
looking for those who just want to hang out. He's looking for commitment. Sadly, many people go through

their entire lives liking Jesus but never really committing. This isn't a new concept, and it's not surprising to Jesus.

In Matthew 7:21–23, Jesus clarified what it means to follow Him. He explained that people can say and do good things, can even appear very religious, yet still not know Him. Jesus said, "Many will say to me on that day, 'Lord, Lord, did we not prophesy in your name and in your name drive out demons and in your name perform many miracles?' Then I will tell them plainly, 'I never knew you. Away from me, you evildoers!'" Remember, Jesus was not teaching to the "down-and-outers"; He was teaching those who were somehow making a show of their religion—an outward appearance without an authentic and personal relationship with Him.

Jesus isn't looking for people who want to associate with His name as a way to do good deeds or to be part of a club. He wants people who truly want to know Him in a deep and personal way. He's not looking for people to acknowledge Him. He's looking for people to *receive* Him in a committed, "follow Me" relationship.

THE OFFER

One of the remarkable aspects of Christian faith is that this relationship with Jesus is always an offer. It is never forced. Love is this way. It is always an offer. Real love is never forced. We are free to say yes or no to Jesus. For every Simon Peter and Andrew and Levi in the Bible, there are those who will decide not to follow.

Once a young man ran up to Jesus, asking what he needed to "do" to inherit eternal life (Mark 10:17–22). As Jesus often did, He led the conversation to allow this man to see himself clearly. Jesus is a master of understanding the human heart—indeed, the Bible clarifies that Jesus "knew what was in each person" (John 2:25)—and it's clear in this story that He understood exactly what this young man needed.

So Jesus didn't even ask this earnest guy a question. He just began listing out Jewish commandments, and the young man interjected, "Yes, yes, I've kept all of those!" But what happens next is most interesting. Mark 10:21 says, "Jesus looked at him and loved him."

Jesus looked. He didn't preach a sermon. He didn't point fingers. He didn't even engage in a Q&A about eternal life. Instead, He looked directly at this young man and turned the full attention of His heart and mind upon this person, inviting him to engage in a relationship. For us, as for this man, the temptation is always to look for a set of rules to follow that will tell us if we are "good" enough for whatever we desire to attain. But this is nowhere near what Jesus does; in fact, He does the exact opposite. Jesus fixes His gaze upon this young man, and He sees who he really is.

Jesus loved. It was in the looking that love developed. It wasn't in the young man's stringent keeping of the rules or in the amazing deeds. Jesus looked and loved him just for being himself. Can you imagine having the full force of Jesus's attention and love focused in your direction?

It's clear that the young man really liked *the idea* of Jesus and wanted to make a good choice. But when Jesus made the offer for relationship, He did so in the context of full commitment: "Go, sell your possessions and give to the poor, and you will have treasure in heaven. Then come, follow me" (Matthew 19:21). When Jesus looked and loved this man, He knew exactly what He needed to ask him to reveal his true heart. This young man thought he was doing everything right and had it all together. But like all of us, he had some blind spots in his own life. By pressing the issue of possessions, Jesus cut right to the heart of the matter for this particular individual.

So Jesus looked at him, loved him, and laid before him a choice for relationship. And get this—the young man walked away. This is the surprise of God. God obviously holds all the power in a relationship with each of us, but surprisingly, He gives us the freedom to say yes or no to Him. Such is love.

We have the freedom to say yes or no to God's offer of relationship.

Love, to be love, always comes as an offer. Sometimes people say, "If God wants all of us to have a relationship with Him, why didn't He just preprogram us so we would?" Good question, but love cannot be preprogrammed; it cannot be forced, or it wouldn't be love. If we were forced to say yes to Jesus, forced to become Christians, this would go against the grain of God's character and the central theme of Christianity—mainly that Jesus's offer is based on love, the purest form of love. This means that Jesus's offer comes with no strings attached, without coercion or manipulation of any kind.

Just last week, Andy, a member of our church staff, made plans to ask his girlfriend to marry him. The proposal was elaborate—with many moving parts and people. Many friends were involved in the plan that he put together. But when we wanted to know how the proposal had gone, we didn't ask about any of the elaborate plans. We first wanted to know, "Did she say yes?" The main thing was whether his girlfriend would say yes to marriage—because despite the great lengths that he put into place, she was still free to say yes or no.

It's been said that the only thing God wants that He cannot give Himself is your love. If He forced us into it, it wouldn't be love. The freedom to say yes or no, despite the great lengths that God has gone to bring us to Himself, is what makes our relationship joyful to God, and it is what makes it joyful to us. To give the offer and to receive a yes is what's thrilling. Which is why Andy's text message after we asked, "Did she say yes?" was, "I'm so excited!"

THE WAY TO LOVE

So how does Jesus offer Himself to us? What's the way of His proposal? Stunningly, the offer is Jesus's dying on the cross. Jesus offers His life for every person in the world, including you. God: the source of all life. God: who is love. The ultimate expression of that love: Jesus's sacrifice. Death on a cross.

When you think about this exchange—Jesus's life so we might have a relationship with God—you might be shocked. *Why? Why a gruesome death? Why is it necessary for someone to be humiliated, to be beaten, and to suffer for me? Isn't there another way?* If you're thinking this, you're in good company. A man named Paul, who wrote much of the New Testament, said in a letter to one of the early churches, "I know very well how foolish [the message of the cross] sounds" (1 Corinthians 1:18 TLB). Even the men inspired by God to write Scripture knew that the cross would offend our sensibilities about the nice way to be in relationship with one another. So the cross is where we leave our earthly expressions of love behind and enter into an entirely different kind of relationship.

WHY THE CROSS?

Even as we write this, we can hear the protests from friends who are seeking life in God. When we open up our minds to this reality—this necessary exchange as Jesus's incredible offer to us—it sets our minds spinning. This is where a reminder might be in order. Remember when you picked up this book? You did so because something was stirring in you—a God stirring. Remember when we reminded you that it's not about *all of this* but about this man, that it starts with Jesus? When you settle your heart back into this place, perhaps you remember that Jesus's offer of freedom and life is incredibly appealing. The offer of a new start, of forgiveness, of a way to a new life is so appealing because of the truth within us that understands something is just not right. And that place—the place of dissonance within you—is where we can focus again on the way to love. That way to love starts with the problem of our sin and God's answer to that problem: the cross.

SIN?

Put simply, sin is anything in us that is not perfectly pure. *C'mon, you gotta be kidding!* you might think. *Everyone has stuff in them that's not perfectly pure.* Exactly. This is why the Bible says, "All have sinned and fall short of the glory of God" (Romans 3:23). At the deepest level, we recognize that all is not right within us. Perhaps this is the part of us interested in responding to a God stirring. There might be big ways in your life you've experienced this lack of wholeness or pureness, or maybe it's more subtle. Whether it's a series of events or a train of thoughts, we recognize that all is not right.

Some people think sin is not these little pinpricks of conviction, but only the "big stuff," like murder. So if sin is just things like murder, most people think, *I don't have a problem with sin.* True enough, if sin was only about the big stuff. The challenge here is that we are talking about having a relationship with God, and God is perfectly pure in all respects.

To have a relationship with Him means that we too must become pure. If God welcomed our sin—if He accepted anything in us that was less than pure, if He kind of winked at it and looked the other way—then God Himself wouldn't be pure. He'd be a corrupt guy who winks at wrong, a kind of mafia boss. That's not the God we're talking about, not God the Father of Jesus Christ, not God the Creator of everything, about whom we're told, "God is light; in him there is no darkness at all" (1 John 1:5). Another word for this purity of God, this light without any darkness, is holiness.

When I (Nicole) was little, my family stopped by the Grand Canyon during a cross-country move. I don't remember much about that trip, but I remember two things about seeing the Grand Canyon for the first time. First, it was so magnificent that it felt like time stopped. Seeing the sheer size—the depth and the breadth of the canyon—caused everything else in me and around me to fade away. Second, it was silent. Something about the magnitude of the canyon and the awe of its beauty caused everyone to stop chattering about lunch plans or picture taking. Anyone who looked out toward the canyon became still and quiet, drawn into the wonder of its scope and beauty.

This is my best understanding of God's holiness. When we encounter a breathtaking view or a moment so beautiful that it makes time stop and our voices go quiet, we are getting close to God's holiness. His holiness is overwhelming; it's magnificent and perspective shaking. His holiness is what makes God *God*. So when we start to consider His way of leading us into a relationship with Him, we must remember that ordinary never stands a chance against holy—because His holiness is pure, and to come close to that holiness requires us to be pure as well.

So God—Creator of the Grand Canyon and Creator of us—wants this relationship with us. The whole story of the Bible and the story of all the people who experienced God stirrings are about God wanting to know them, wanting to love them, wanting to be in a relationship with them. But since sin keeps us from it—keeps us from being pure enough to be near His holiness—this relationship requires a standard that's impossible for us to meet. In ourselves we cannot meet it; we "fall short," just as the verse says. God alone is the one who can address this gap between us.

Jesus—in His perfect life and His willing, sacrificial death—makes up the difference. He is the solution to the problem and the difference maker in our lives.

The Bible calls Jesus a reconciler (Colossians 1:20), because He reconciles our sin with God's holiness by His death on the cross. Because God is holy, because in Him there is no darkness at all, and because God is just—because He cannot and will not look away from sin, wink at it, ignore the ramifications of the way sin causes trouble and strife—Jesus's death was necessary. Jesus was pure in every aspect, one who had "no sin" (2 Corinthians 5:21), and He willingly took all our sin, the burden of it, and the penalty of it upon Himself to create that reconciliation between God's holiness and our impurity.

Here's another way to think of sin: Have you ever said something unkind behind someone's back that he or she later found out about? If you are particularly nice, maybe you'll have to think back to middle school. But think about that time when the one you offended confronted you. You knew that person was right and you'd been caught. If you can recall that moment, you probably remember feeling the weight of your wrongness press upon your heart, and you felt trapped, caught, ashamed. Those moments are weighty. They breach the trust of someone who thought you were kind but just discovered you weren't. These moments are also costly because they are a reminder to you about who you really can be. Mean. Selfish. Impure.

Even when trapped with the truth, we wonder if we can find a way out without having to confess. Perhaps we look for a way to justify ourselves or blame someone else. We try to reconcile the incident in our own way—by justification or by shifting blame or by making excuses. And it really doesn't work that well.

Now imagine if that moment wasn't about one thing you said but about a lifetime of wrongdoing, a lifetime of character flaws and self-serving judgments and attitudes. No wonder the Bible says Jesus "bore our sins" (1 Peter 2:24), because dealing with even the "smallest" of sin is burdensome. And no wonder it says that Jesus "endured the cross, scorning its shame" (Hebrews 12:2), because sin creates pain and shame in us. This is the why of the cross—why our sin has a cost, and why Jesus was the one who was willing, in His love, to take that upon Himself. Jesus in His love, the sinless Son of God[1] bore the costly weight of

. . . .

1   "God made him who had no sin to be sin for us, so that in him
     we might become the righteousness of God" (2 Corinthians
     5:21).

our wrongdoing, to do for us what we cannot do for ourselves—to make us pure.

Imagine the magnitude of this: someone gave His life for us as an expression of love, to the point where He indeed died for us. Then imagine that after observing *all of this,* we say, "No, thanks. Not interested." It's stunning that we could do such a thing. Stunning that the person would love so much and risk so much and pour Himself out in complete vulnerability … knowing that we might say no to His sacrifice. This is the essence of how it works with Jesus's offer to us. He gave everything, including His life, knowing that many will say, "No, thanks. Not interested." There on a cross He died, vulnerable, offering the entirety of Himself. And because the offer is an offer of love, we are free to say yes or no to Him—to a personal relationship with the God of love.

So now we've talked about this God stirring within you, we've talked about the *all of this*, and we've talked about what Jesus is offering through His sacrifice: the way to new life, to forgiveness and a relationship with God. And now let's say we've come to the place where we would like this new life in a relationship with God—but one more thing has to happen.

GETTING HONEST

One of the important aspects of a committed relationship is disclosure. Remember back in Genesis when
God asked, "Where are you?" That's a question to
restore transparency. If you read further in Genesis 3,
we see that Adam and Eve were hiding from Him. No
relationship can thrive if hiding is involved.

Here's where our dating analogy comes back into
play. Part of the dating phase is the process of getting
to know each other. For a relationship to work well,
two people will need to know the honest truth about
each other. This comes over time—over conversations,
over experiences together, over listening to each other,
over sharing hearts. For the relationship to be healthy,
this listening to each other has to include a kind of full
disclosure—both the nice stuff and the not-so-nice
stuff about ourselves. Without this, the relationship
would be manipulative or deceptive. That doesn't
work well for human relationships, and it doesn't work
well with Jesus.

Let's say two people are on a first date and go
out for a long dinner. One says to the other, "Tell me
about yourself. Where are you from, what do you like
to do, stuff like that?" In response the other person tells
about where she grew up, talks a little bit about her

family life, her growing-up years, and then the things she enjoys in life. Great. Then that person returns the question, "Well, I've shared about me … what about you?" Then the other person says, "No, I don't want you to know about me." What? How weird! And after more probing, the person still refuses to disclose anything. You know where that relationship is headed after that one date? Nowhere!

This idea of mutual transparency and disclosure is a simple one we almost don't even think about because it's so basic to the formation of relationships. And while we aren't likely to tell our deepest stuff on the first date (that could be kind of weird too), in time—if we are going to enter a truly committed relationship, one that grows deep—we'll want to know the full story about the other person. A true and real and healthy relationship will never form without this. Risky? Yes. But that's part of real relationships.

So if we are talking about a relationship with Jesus, and it's going to be healthy and real, then we have to enter it with full disclosure. In a relationship with Jesus, "full disclosure" is when we confess the truth about ourselves to Him. And since He's not an ordinary person but He is God's Son, this disclosure is confessing our sin to Him. This is because He alone can give us complete forgiveness, and this experience of complete honesty and complete forgiveness is what makes our relationship with Jesus so special. It's also what makes it real. This is the process of "receiving" Him.

TO ALL WHO RECEIVE JESUS ...

To all who did receive him, to those who believed in his name, he gave the right to become children of God.
John 1:12

The word *receive* is rich with meaning. To *receive* a package from a delivery person means you hold out your hands while the person reaches the package forward to you. Your hands are in "receive" mode. The other person is the initiator, and you are the receiver. To receive is to be humble and open to another—to place yourself in "receivership."

Here's another use of the word *receive*: "Would you be willing to *receive* some advice about how you handled that meeting at work yesterday?" This question could trigger all sorts of responses. If you are going to actually receive the advice (rather than sit back with your arms crossed and dismiss what the person is saying), you have to be humble and have to "open yourself" to "take in" what the person offers. Advice is like that—it's an offer for the humble. The humble receive it; the proud don't.

To *receive* a package, to *receive* advice, is to open yourself to take in what is being presented and offered. Actually taking it in is something quite different from just participating in the exercise. You can "accept" a package by leaving it unopened by the front door— but you aren't actually "receiving" it.

You know that you can "participate" in a conversation where you are given advice without actually "receiving" the advice. You can nod appreciatively, all the while knowing that you reject in your heart what is being said. You went through the motions, you appeared to be interested, but in your heart you rejected it. Many people do this with Christianity. They go through the motions, they may nod appreciatively, but in their hearts they do not actually "take it in"—they do not "receive it," nor do they "open themselves" to Jesus. Millions of people like this fill thousands of churches around the world. They are going through the motions but have never received Jesus.

Similar to this scenario is the difference between "acknowledging" God rather than actually receiving Him. There's a subtle but crucially important difference between these two concepts. To acknowledge God is in a sense to nod to Him. Perhaps we give assent to Him. There may be a God-concept in our lives; we may have gone to church for years based on this. We may have sung songs, prayed prayers, and listened to sermons. Acknowledging God in this way, we developed a kind of "religion habit" and fully believed that we were "doing the right God thing."

This practice of religion is acknowledging God by having an external engagement with Him. In this practice, God remains a concept rather than a personal and living relationship. God may "teach us some good things about life" or "be good for my kids to know about," but one way or another we have kept Him distant, outside of ourselves. We place God safely on a shelf, like He's a library reference book that we go to when the occasion or the religious holiday warrants. This external engagement of acknowledging God is quite different from "receiving" Him. The Bible doesn't say "to all who acknowledged Him, He gave the right to become children of God," but "to all who did *receive* him … he gave the right to become children of God" (John 1:12).

To receive Him is to "take Him in," and this makes all the difference. Now God is inside rather than outside; He is present rather than distant—I have a relationship with Him rather than an arrangement with Him. If I only acknowledge God, He is impersonal, distant, and stagnant. If I receive God, He is personal, present, and life-giving.

Along these lines, to receive someone is to accept that person in your heart. Herein is the core matter of our relationship with Jesus—the core question: "Do I *receive* Jesus Christ?" You may have been "following" Him for a while, and now the relationship seems to be asking for a new step: "What's this relationship about? Where is it headed? What are your intentions? Do you wish for commitment, or are you just dabbling, just hanging out?"

To *receive* Jesus, I would have to be at a level where I feel comfortable enough and I trust Him enough to begin this committed relationship. And here the metaphor used in the Bible expands to include both marriage and adoption. As we've seen, John 1:12 begins, "To all who did *receive* him," and then continues, "to those who believed in his name, he gave the right to become children of God." Now the fullest type of relationship is at hand. It's committed, like a marriage, and it's bringing you into the family, like an adoption.

To become a Christian is to begin this relationship by *receiving* Jesus Christ. It includes full disclosure, it includes the humility to be in the receiving position, and it includes actually taking Him in. This happens when we pray and sincerely tell Jesus Christ that we want this relationship—for real, with commitment. If you want that, praying a simple and true prayer is how it begins: God, I want a relationship with You. I confess my sin and ask You to forgive me through Jesus. And now I invite You, Jesus, into my life as my Lord and my Savior, forever. Amen.

When you pray this prayer with a sincere desire for a relationship with Him, when you come to the place where you say yes to Jesus's offer of a relationship— you've begun. You've started a new life with Him. You've also done something more. You've received a new identity, which we'll talk about next.

So this is Jesus's offer to us. It is the ultimate offer: His life given for our life. It is an offer that every person can say yes or no to. Jesus giving His life for ours is both the offer and the way we enter into a relationship with God. It's hard to believe that He would do this on the chance that people might say no to the offer. But that's what love does. He has given His life—not just His affections, but His very life as the way for us to have a relationship with God. And because it's an offer, we can respond as we wish. Such is love. Imagine.

Chapter 4

WHAT JUST HAPPENED?

· ·

Dana Humbert, grad student, age twenty-six

This all started when I hit a breaking point: where every terrible thing that could happen, did. My longtime boyfriend and I broke up. I had been having residual feelings for another man for about a year, and I consistently lied to my boyfriend about it, which spurred the demise of our relationship. I destroyed my ankle during a soccer game, so I was completely incapacitated—and I didn't have health insurance. I realized I did not want to continue on with my grad program after preparing for four years in undergrad for this career. I had no idea what I wanted to do with my life—twenty-three and not a single idea.

I felt alone and abandoned and unworthy of anyone's love. I think I would say that in this time of turmoil, the process of being stirred by God was quite sudden. But looking back, God was planting a seed, and there were so many opportunities that presented themselves when He was reaching out to me. The terrible things that I experienced, that I did, or that just occurred, all happened for a reason. My injury led me to begin physical therapy to rehabilitate my ankle—and I found out I wanted to be a physical therapist. My broken relationship helped me realize that I need to depend on only one man in my life for unconditional love and support—and it's not any earthly man.

It's hard to explain how God stirred in me except to say that He did. I know He did—not through any person or church, but just with Him and me. A few months later, my mom invited me to come to a church with her, but at that moment it was really God rescuing me. At first, I had a hard time accepting God's love. For months, I had felt this indescribable guilt in the deepest parts of my soul. What kind of God loves a person who lied the way I did? How could I be forgiven for what I had done—for the pain I had caused another human being? I couldn't accept God's love for me. I felt ashamed. I felt terrible whenever I heard others talk about their guilt because it seemed like the things they had done were small compared to what I had done. I felt unworthy of anything; I felt that I deserved to be unhappy. I had made my bed, and I deserved to lie in it. I was longing to be happy with someone, anyone. When you experience darkness like that in your life, you feel like there is no power, no person, nothing that can save you from yourself. But when I began to open up to the possibility that God wanted to love me and forgive me, my life started to change.

I started feeling overwhelmed with gratitude, and I still do. Deep in my heart now, I feel so grateful, and that stays with me every minute of every day.

Right now I'm trying to understand Jesus more—who He was, what He said, what He did, and why He had to die. I told a friend the other day, "I feel like a God-stian—not so much a Christian—because I understand God but not Christ." I'm trying to go back to the basics of Christianity and my faith and get acclimated. When you don't have a good understanding of the basics of Christianity, you feel like you're just aimlessly wandering around without a map. I haven't arrived, but I'm well on the journey with Him now.

If anyone is in Christ, he is a new creation. The old has passed away; behold the new has come.
2 Corinthians 5:17 ESV

We've all received gifts over our lifetimes, but some are more memorable than others. The most memorable gift I (Nicole) ever received was thirteen years ago on Valentine's Day. For my husband, Dave, and me, the Valentine's Day routine is mostly, well, routine. Maybe a nice card and a dinner out during that week. We aren't prone to much sentimentality, which made this particular Valentine's Day so memorable.

I walked in from work that day to find a card on the counter. Inside that card was a little riddle and clue, which led me to our guest-room closet. Here I found a gift: a new stereo for my office. Dave knew how much I loved listening to music during work. But even more intriguing was another card inside of that gift. That card led to another place in the house and another thoughtful gift. I skipped through the house like a little girl on Christmas Day, tearing wrapping paper off one gift, then reading clues and searching for the next.

At the end of it all, I had five gifts in my hands. The reason the day was memorable wasn't because the gifts were the biggest or most extravagant Dave has ever purchased for me. It was the extra lengths he went through to give them that made me feel so loved and special. The gifts were specially suited to me. There was a spirit of adventure and fun as I took delight in one present after the next. If you asked Dave what the best gift was that he's ever bought for me, he would *know* it was this one, because I'm still talking about it to this day.

One of the things I love about Dave is his fun-loving attitude toward things like our relationship. But when it comes to starting a relationship with God, we might get the impression that life with God isn't like a loving relationship at all. People may give us the impression that becoming a Christian is when we really "start following the rules" or get serious about life. We might think that all the fun will be sucked out of us because we won't be doing anything bad anymore—after all, we've gotten religious.

But there couldn't be anything further from the truth. Yes, a relationship with God is pretty big, just like a marriage. But starting a relationship with God is like unwrapping one gift after another. We don't lose in this arrangement; we gain! At first glance, we might not even know we need the gifts that our heavenly Father has prepared for us. But as we step into this life, we'll find that the gifts God gives us reach into the deepest places of our hearts and satisfy our deepest needs. As we walk forward into the adventure of life with God, we will look back on our life without Him, and it won't seem like "more fun." It will seem dreary, flat, bleak. Beginning a relationship with God is like Dorothy stepping out of the black-and-white landscape of Kansas into a glorious, vibrant life in Oz. Numerous friends have described their lives before a relationship with Jesus like living in "black and white"—and life after starting a relationship with Him like being in color.

This is the good news of a relationship with God. When we receive Christ, we receive many new gifts. We unwrap one after another, amazed at how our heavenly Father knows so well the contours of our hearts, the needs of our souls. These gifts make us feel known, cherished, loved. These gifts—the promises of God that we have access to through Christ—are starting points, the building blocks for our new lives with Him. Now we're going to talk about some of these gifts.

NEW ETERNITY

God is life, and God lives forever. When you pray to begin a relationship with Jesus Christ, you have begun a new life in God. Coming to life in Him, or "feeling really alive for the first time," is a gift from God's Spirit—an enormous joy as we come alive in God. Indeed, in the Bible it is God's Spirit, the Holy Spirit, who is always bringing things to life. He was present at the earliest moments of creation, where the Bible tells us "the Spirit of God was hovering over the waters" (Genesis 1:2). This hovering is a metaphor describing the way an eagle hovers over her nest, flapping her wings above her new hatchlings, invigorating them with rushing air and drying their feathers so they can transition from their prehatched stage to their new-life stage. In a sense, she is bringing them to life and empowering them to live. It's a beautiful picture of the Holy Spirit, who you might say is a specialist in life giving. The Holy Spirit is sometimes called "the shy member of the Trinity."[1] He usually doesn't take a front-row seat in God's work, but He is always empowering and giving life. In the New Testament, we learn that at the resurrection of Jesus, it was the Holy Spirit who "raised Jesus from the dead" (Romans 8:11). Giving life and empowering us for living—these are the beautiful work of the Holy Spirit, who ancient teachings describe as "the Lord and Giver of Life."[2]

When the Holy Spirit helps us come to life in a personal relationship with God, we enter eternal life, and our sins are completely forgiven. The gospel of John says it this way: "I tell you the truth, those who listen to my message and believe in God who sent me have eternal life. They will never be condemned for their sins, but they have already passed from death into life" (John 5:24 NLT). It's big, but it's also clear: you've begun eternal life, and your sin is forgiven. Forever. Past, present, future. The Bible is clear that there will come a day when we will all give account for

....

1   Frederick Dale Bruner and William Hordern coined this phrase in *The Holy Spirit: Shy Member of the Trinity* (Eugene, OR: Wipf & Stock Publishers, 2001).

2   From the Nicene Creed, www.creeds.net/ancient/nicene.htm.

our lives (Romans 14:12). But when you receive Jesus, you will not be condemned. Not now, not later.

Additionally, now that you've entered into a relationship with the God who is eternal life, you, too, have entered eternal life. *But I'm still going to die*, you're thinking. Yes, physically your body will die, but your soul—the essence of your being—will not die. It will live with God forever. *You* will live with God forever. That's why Jesus said "he has *passed from* death into life." The reality of your eternity was changed once you entered a relationship with the One who is eternal life. Your death is not the reality of your eternity. Death is only the conclusion of your earthly body's physical functioning. In a very real way, it is not an ending but a transition to the next way of life for which God created you.

This concept is sometimes hard for us to grasp because we live in a world that emphasizes the physical over the spiritual, the material over the immaterial. Generally this means that when you think of "you," you think of your body. You "see yourself" in your mind as though you are looking in a mirror—which is to say, you have a picture of what your physical appearance looks like. But the essence of "you" is not a body; it's your soul. We must emphasize this again because it flies in the face of what we are taught in our culture. A part of us is eternal, and that part of us is the core of our being—our spirit or soul.

Interestingly, even modern science is taking note of the inconsistencies in current theories of life, which reduce humanity to a pool of genes, evolution, and random circumstance. Robert Lanza, a scientist some herald as "a modern-day Einstein" and upon whom the film *Good Will Hunting* was based, has even developed a modern scientific theory of the universe that points to evidence of a part of humanity that "is immortal and exists outside of time and space."[3]

For those of us who were raised outside of a tradition of faith, just shifting our perspective to include the concept of a soul can be mind-blowing! If you aren't sure where you stand on that, consider these questions: When someone you've known has died, what have you thought happens to him or her next? Have you ever given it much thought—not just in a clichéd way, but honestly?

It can sometimes take an unusually tragic circumstance to make us begin to ask those questions. But

. . . .

3   Robert Lanza, "Does the Soul Exist? Evidence Says 'Yes,'" *Psychology Today*, December 21, 2011, www.psychologytoday.com/blog/biocentrism/201112/does-the-soul-exist-evidence-says-yes.

when we get close to the line between life and death, we find these questions very important, and this matter of our soul becomes paramount.

"It is the soul that has a body, not the body that has a soul."[4] Everything shifts when we realize that we are a soul, that we are surrounded by souls, and that the conclusion of our body's earthly life is not the conclusion of "us." Understanding ourselves first as souls puts a new perspective on what our true needs are. Often when we think of what we need, we summon up ideas that are physical and temporary. *I need food, water, sleep. I need a vacation, a new pair of shoes, a new hobby.* But Jesus consistently taught His followers that their greatest needs were not physical but spiritual. Spiritual needs like *I need assurance in the face of pain; I need peace that transcends and often contradicts my circumstances; I need perspective on what really matters.* And Jesus, who called Himself the "living water" and the "bread of life," made it clear that we need *Him*—yes, our souls need *Him* as desperately as our bodies need bread and water. You see, without understanding our eternal existence, we lose perspective on our greatest needs. We reduce the

---

4   William Walsham How, *Plain Words to Children* (London: W. Wells Gardner, 1878), 29.

full scope of what it means to be human to a one-dimensional story.

I (David) recently shared an illustration when teaching about heaven. So many people found it helpful as a way to grasp the reality of eternity that we wanted to share it with you here:

> In a mother's womb were twin babies. One asked the other: "Do you believe in life after delivery?"
>
> The other replies, "Why, of course. There has to be something after delivery. Maybe we are here to prepare ourselves for what we will be later."
>
> "Nonsense," says the other. "There is no life after delivery. What would that life be?"
>
> "I don't know, but there will be more light than here. Maybe we will walk with our legs and eat from our mouths."
>
> The other said, "This is absurd! Walking is impossible. And eat with our mouths? Ridiculous. The

umbilical cord supplies nutrition. Life after delivery is to be excluded. The umbilical cord is too short."

"I think there is something, and maybe it's different than it is here."

The other twin replies, "No one has ever come back from there. Delivery is the end of life, and in the after-delivery it is nothing but darkness and anxiety—and it takes us nowhere."

"Well, I don't know," says the other, "but certainly we will see Mother, and she will take care of us."

"Mother? You believe in a Mother?" replies the twin. "But where is she now?"

"She is all around us. It is in her that we live. Without her there would not be this world."

"I don't see her, so it's only logical that she doesn't exist."

To which the other replied, "Sometimes when you're in silence you can hear her, you can perceive her. I believe there is a reality after delivery, and we are here to prepare ourselves for that reality."[5]

So this eternal life began for you when you prayed to receive Jesus. And God has made you a new creation. Your earthly life now is a matter of growing into what He's made for eternal purposes. Just as the womb prepares us for earthly life, so also does this earthly life prepare us for eternal life. Talk about perspective shifting! Imagine thinking about the stress of your job, your relational angst, your resentment toward an old friend … imagine thinking of all those things in light of eternity—maybe even as preparation for it! Changes things, doesn't it? With our new eternity also comes the next gift of life with God: an identity makeover.

TRUE IDENTITY

Have you ever had to show your driver's license to someone? I bet when you did, you said (or wanted to say) something like, "That's really not a good picture of me. It was a bad picture day." Almost all people dislike their picture on their driver's license. But …

....

5   "Life after Delivery"; widely available on the Internet, original source unknown.

that's what you actually look like. Or at least it's what you actually looked like the moment that picture was taken. For better or worse, cameras don't lie. They simply show exactly what's there. So here's some bad news for you; the picture on your driver's license actually looks like you! Sorry. That's tough news for most of us who are constantly trying to improve our identity, at least in the eyes of other people. We want them to think highly of us. What does this say about us or suggest about us?

The point here is that most of us have identity insecurity. We would like to look better, and we'd like to be better. Most of us with some life experience would like to have better character; we'd like to be smarter, prettier, more accomplished. You get the picture. These desires to be better, more admired, more _____ (you can fill in the word here) come from identity insecurity, or what we would call "identity deficits." These insecurities and deficits are the result of factors that are so numerous it would be foolish to try to name them all. In general, though, they come from things like the way we were treated when we were young—we may have had a parent who made us feel that we were never enough. Or we may have done things in our lives that give us a sense of regret. They linger in our memories;

they cause us to have a lower sense of self, a lower sense of identity than we would like. We'd like to be more admired, more loved, more cherished. You could say we feel "deficits" of love, of admiration, of being cherished; and we feel, think, and act out of these deficits, always trying to find ways to cover over or fill or disguise these places where we feel "less than."

That is the pre-Jesus reality of everyone. Yet when we enter into our new identity in a relationship with Jesus, we find that the deepest longings of our hearts are beginning to be met in new and unexpected ways. Remember how Heather said it in the beginning of chapter 3: "Accepting Christ and choosing to follow Him and feeling the warmth of His love and acceptance was the first time I felt like I was in the in crowd."

The Bible says that when you received Jesus Christ, God gave you the right to a new identity—your identity as a child of God: "See what great love the Father has lavished on us, that we should be called children of God!" (1 John 3:1).

In John 1:12, we read that through Jesus, God gave us "the right to become children of God." The phrase "right to become" is worded like a legal statement: the words that describe the transaction of adoption. God has adopted you into His family; you have become His daughter, His son. In both verses (John 1:12 and 1 John 3:1) and throughout the Bible, we hear two consistent themes: God's deep love for us and His desire to be in relationship with us. It's because of His love that He adopts us into His family. It's His love that gives us the right to be in this kind of close relationship with Him!

My (Nicole's) youngest brother was adopted into our family when I was seven. I can remember standing at Kennedy Airport in New York, nose pressed against the glass, shoulder to shoulder with my other siblings. The lights of the plane slowly descended, and after what felt like hours, footsteps sounded through the long tunnel toward the terminal. I will never forget gazing down that long hallway, watching stoic Korean women parade forward, each carrying a baby toward the waiting parents-to-be. The terminal became a delivery room that day, because when Stevie was placed into my parents' arms, it was a rebirth. Yes, he had already been born—but it wasn't until that moment that he was born again—born into his "forever family" as many adoption agencies like to say.

Almost thirty years later, Stevie is still working to grasp what this rebirth means to him. He recently sent me an email explaining how his life has been shaped by adoption:

It was hard for me to see that I was really part of this family despite the ethnicity difference, but I've learned that you have only one family and need to love and cherish them for eternity. I love this family, and I love the person I came to be. If it wasn't for all of you guys sticking with me through the darkest tunnels and the deepest holes, I wouldn't be who I am. It took me many years to find who I was, and I have no regrets about any of this. God worked a wonder in my life and helped me realize that nothing is more important than the family you have.

When I think about Stevie saying, "Nothing is more important than the family you have," I completely agree. But in God's economy, our rebirth is into *His* family, headed by a perfect, loving Father. Never once did we think of Stevie as just partially in our family, *despite the fact that Stevie struggled to accept his adoption.* You can never be half-adopted or half-born. In the spiritual sense, most of us are like Stevie. It may take us some time of questioning and growing before we even begin to fully grasp what a rebirth—new life, new identity—really means.

We have found over the years that this insecurity is something that many Christians feel. They ask things like, "How do I really know I'm a Christian?" "How do I really (really, really) know that God accepts me and that I am truly His child?" Remember 1 John 3:1: "See what great love the Father has lavished on us, that we should be called children of God!" Similar to the essence of adoption, it's the parent's love and sacrifice—not the child's lineage or DNA—that bring the child into a new family. Likewise in our spiritual adoption, it's God's love and sacrifice, not our lineage or DNA, that make us His children. Some Christians struggle with this their whole lives. But God doesn't want it to be that way. God wants you to know that through Jesus, you have really, *really* become His child. To help us, God has left us with specific ways we can know Him and embrace our new identity in His family, and that is helpful to us as we attempt to live into this truth. We'll talk more about that in chapter 6.

NEW IDENTITY

The right to become God's children is made possible by Jesus, and the incredible news is that because of Jesus, God now says the same thing about us—His sons and daughters—that He said about Jesus. Ready for it? Here you go: "This is my Son, whom I love; with him I am well pleased" (Matthew 3:17). Even more personally, in Mark 1:11 the Bible depicts it this way: "*You* are my Son, whom I love; with you I am well pleased." In *The Message*, author Eugene Peterson rendered it as, "This is my Son, chosen and marked by my love, delight of my life."[6]

Right now, we invite you to take a break from reading to reflect on this. Because of Jesus, God says the same thing about you that He said about Jesus: "You are My son (or daughter), whom I love, and with you I am well pleased." Imagine God, the Father, the Creator of the universe, who knew you before you were born, saying *your* name.

"_____, you are My son (or daughter), whom I love, and with you I am well pleased."

"_____, you are My son (or daughter), chosen and marked by My love, pride of My life."

Take a minute right now to receive that; take it in. Talk to God about this. If you're beginning to understand it, you probably just want to say, "Thank You! Thank You! Thank You!"

In this one statement, God gives us an incredible supply of affirmation for the identity deficits that we all feel—that gnawing, deep craving for belonging,

....

6   See longer reference for *The Message* in this book's Further Reading section.

love, and approval. Note the three distinct elements in this statement of promise:

1. You are My son.
2. Whom I love.
3. With you I am well pleased.

You Are My Son

When God says, "You are My son," He is identifying Himself with us. He is saying that He wants to be associated with us, that we are together. This is the opposite of the way we sometimes distance ourselves from someone whom we find unappealing. Think of how a husband and wife might talk to each other when their child is misbehaving. In a playful (or not-so-playful) way, the husband might say to the wife, "Your son is misbehaving; I think you need to do something about him." There is a subtle desire to disassociate from the child because of the child's poor behavior. If you're married with kids, you know how this goes; you've probably said it a time or two. What you're saying—hopefully in jest—is, "That's not *my* child behaving like that! I think you need to do something about *your* son!" If you are unhappy with someone who is close to you, you tend to disassociate yourself from that person. This happens with siblings, too, like when you're in high school and your kid sister acts ridiculous and one of your friends says, "Isn't that *your* sister?" Embarrassed by her behavior, you'd rather not claim that she is in fact your sister. Half-kidding (or maybe with some real frustration), you say something like, "No way; that's not *my* sister!"

Point number one of this new identity is that we are people with whom God is pleased to be associated. He's saying, "Yep, that's My daughter; that's My son." He never dissociates Himself from us once we have become His children. Pretty flattering that He'd be so kind, despite our sometimes lousy behavior!

Whom I Love

Sometimes in a family relationship, we might not always like each other, let alone love each other. If you have a family member whom you don't like, you might feel, *Yes, I have to claim that he's my brother, but I don't like him.* It would be devastating to think that one of your parents doesn't actually love you. Many of us spend years of our adult lives trying to recover from a deep sense that we were not loved or approved of by a parent. Perhaps you know what this feels like.

But God is not this way. Not only is God saying, "Yes, that's My son," but He's also claiming, "I *love* this son. He has My affection. My heart is *with* him and it's *for* him." Now our love-starved souls can know that the God of the universe announces, "We go together." Not only that, but He loves us, and His affections are for us. If your soul is hungry, if you know what identity deficits feel like, understanding that God says these things about you, that He *feels* these things for you, is so satisfying. As we begin to grasp this truth about God, we will begin to feel differently about ourselves. It's incredible what love can do!

With You I Am Well Pleased

God tops off this statement of promise by adding, "I'm so pleased with you." So not only are you His son or daughter, and not only are you His son or daughter for whom He has deep affection and love, but He tops it off by saying, "I'm so proud of you."

God
saying
He's
proud
of
you.

This is very similar to a parent saying, "Yep, that's my daughter. She's awesome, and I'm so proud of her. That's my girl!" The God who set the stars in place is saying that He's pleased with you. He's proud of you. Not of some other person—but *you*.

As we grow into understanding the depth of God's heart for us, these affirmations begin to slowly fill the identity-deficit places in our souls. All those things we've been doing to look for affirmation, to try to be important, to feel important, to be admired, to be thought of highly—now we have an answer. And not from people, not from material things that don't fill our hearts, not from titles or positions … but from God. Once we begin to grasp this new identity and the value and affirmation we are receiving from God Himself, we begin to change—changing and growing by His love.

NEW FAMILY

When we received Jesus Christ, we were adopted into God's family, becoming a son or daughter of God. No longer are we alone in life. No longer are we on our own, by ourselves. Now we know that God is with us and that He will never leave us, never forsake us.

Furthermore, we now share this celebrating fellowship with millions of people who've experienced new life in Jesus Christ. This family is called the church: "all those everywhere who call on the name of the Lord Jesus Christ—their Lord and ours" (1 Corinthians 1:2).

Being in God's family, being a son or daughter of God, has vast implications. This is because what God does for His Son, Jesus, He will do for all His children. He will be with us; He will give life to us; He will raise us from the dead. When we enter into this life, we receive the incredible gift of the Holy Spirit, the life giver (John 6:63). Jesus taught His disciples that the Holy Spirit will be with them (us) forever (John 14:16–17).

Knowing that, we no longer move through life guideless and helpless. We begin to enter a new kind of life, a new way of seeing life, new ways of living it. We now have the confidence and peace of life eternal with God even though our bodies will one day give out. We no longer need to fear death because in a relationship with Jesus Christ, death is transformed. It is not the end; it is a transition, a move, a change. Like birth is to a baby, so will death be to those in Jesus. A wholesale change to a far more expansive and glorious life. Eternal life, with every longing filled, every need for love and affirmation met. No more fear. No more sadness. No more brokenness or broken relationships. No disease. Full joy. And yes, while today we still experience sadness, suffering, loneliness, and longing, the truth of eternity shifts our perspective. We still long and wait and yearn for more, but we know that there will be a day when it all changes, or as J. R. R. Tolkien said, "Everything sad [is] going to come untrue."[7] We experience life differently, not because of a full change in our circumstances, but because of a full change in our perspective. Before, we had only one way to see life: through the lens of self, dimmed by our own selfish needs, our deficits, or our fears, our eyes darting about like a trapped animal. Now, with eternal perspective, we are strengthened to endure the hard times with hope, knowing that there is a reality far beyond the one we are experiencing today.

NEW CHARACTER

When we received Jesus, God's forgiveness was completed in our lives. The offer always existed, but when we received Jesus, we accepted the offer. Just before Jesus died on the cross He declared, "It is finished" (John 19:30). In announcing this, He was saying God's

....

7   J. R. R. Tolkien, *The Return of the King* (New York: Del Rey, 1955, 2012), 246.

work of forgiveness for our sin was completed. This means that our forgiveness is ensured for all time—past, present, and future. You may recall that we defined sin in chapter 3 as "anything in us that is not perfectly pure." Sin is the stuff that was in you before you began to follow Jesus, as well as the ways you'll continue to sin after you follow Him. Those sins—past, present, and future—are the ones He has cast away to make us pure. The Bible says it this way: "As far as the east is from the west, so far has he removed our transgressions from us" (Psalm 103:12).

How far is the east from the west? Where does the east start, and where does the west end? When does the east catch up to the west? This impossibility is God's analogy for the erasing of our sin. Completely gone, completely forgotten. God uses a material impossibility to help us grasp this spiritual reality. This is the gift of being given new character.

So maybe you are thinking, *I don't feel all that different.* Or, *But I am still going to make mistakes; I'm still going to do wrong, to sin.* Yes, you are, and so are we. But God has given us this new standing, this new character as a gift. Our life of growing as a Christian includes growing into this gift, growing into this new standing. God announces our goodness, and as we seek Him, as we unwrap the gifts of this relationship with Him, He grows us into this new gift. He changes us from the inside out, working His truth and His goodness into our character as we receive Him.

Many people find this new character, this new reality too good to be true. Some people think, *This makes it all sound too easy.* This is part of the power of God's grace. Grace means we're given a good thing that we don't deserve. But we'd do well to remember that it wasn't free; it didn't come without a cost. Jesus Christ gave His life so we could have this. Grace is a gift to us, but it was at great cost to God the Father and to Jesus Christ. Many people struggle with grace. Many have a hard time actually believing it, receiving it, making it their own reality. Because of this, many people decide they will somehow punish themselves or do something to "work this off." They might do this by seeking forms of penance (practices to "work off" sin and show God they are taking it seriously), either self-created or presented by a church.

This idea of "paying for our sins" is a deeply ingrained belief that we can work off our own mistakes. In our inner lives, this might come through self-punitive, shaming talk in our heads, where we try to convince God and ourselves that we take our sin seriously. We remind ourselves that we're not good people. We beat ourselves up. We try to find some way to work off our sin.

This mind-set is similar to a bad diet mentality. We try really hard to eat healthy foods, but then the nachos or the gelato or the Oreos get the best of us, and we indulge. We wake up the next morning, resolved that we are serious about our diet, and we "do penance" for our previous night's sin by withholding food. And most of the time, this shame mentality about food just causes us to eat more and more junk the next time we feel hungry or weak. It's a bad spiral.

John Stott, a respected British theologian, once told a story about visiting a friend of his who was a director of a large psychiatric hospital in London. When Stott arrived for the visit, he noted that the hospital was overflowing with patients. When sitting with his friend, Stott asked, "To what do you attribute there being so many patients here? So much need?" The friend was quiet for a moment and then said, "John, half the patients in this hospital could check out tomorrow if they could believe their sins are forgiven."[8]

....

8   John R. W. Stott, *Confess Your Sins* (Philadelphia: Westminster, 1964), 73.

If you have received Jesus, it's true. Your sins are forgiven. The work is finished. There's nothing more for you to do. It's finished.

TOO GOOD TO BE TRUE?

About two years ago, a friend and I (David) got together to talk. This friend was looking for work at the time, and he was also exploring faith in Christ. Eventually the conversation turned to the gift of life and forgiveness through Christ. My friend said to me, "David, I'm not sure I can accept this." I asked him why. He replied, "If it's true, it's just so good. It feels to me that in a way it wouldn't be fair for me to accept something so good when there are so many other people who don't have it." I asked him to describe his feelings further. He said, "This offer is so good, but what about all the other people in the world who don't have it? I don't think I could take this if other people don't have it too." I loved his heart in what he was saying because it indicated that he understood how good the offer truly is. It also indicated that he cared about other people in a sincere way.

"I can appreciate what you are saying," I replied. "And while there's a lot of meaning to what you are saying about other people, that is not your question at this moment. It's a meaningful question, a sincere thought, but it's not your question. The question for you is, how will you respond to Jesus Christ?"

"Yes," he said, "but it doesn't seem fair that I could accept something so good when there are a lot of people who haven't experienced it."

Giving this some thought, I then said to him, "Okay—think of it this way. Over the years as I've been able to travel to a lot of countries, I've seen that there are millions of people around the world who live in poverty. And right now, you've just told me you are looking for a new job. It seems to me that knowing there are millions who live in poverty wouldn't keep you from accepting a job that pays you a good salary. A salary enables you to live in relatively comfortable circumstances when there are millions who have almost nothing. But you would accept a good job right? Seems to me it's a similar idea."

"I get that," he said. "I'll have to think about that."

Maybe you need to think about it too. Working for grace or refusing to accept grace because of our limited understanding of God's nature can be an obstacle, that's for sure. But the question that we posed at the beginning of the book remains. Once again, we have to cut through *all of this* and ask, "What *will you do* with Jesus's offer?" We'd encourage you to say yes to it, and when you do, you are born into a new life, and you receive gifts so great you will need your whole lifetime to begin to comprehend them.

New eternity.

New identity.

New family.

New character.

Grace.

Yes, "if anyone is in Christ, he is a new creation. The old has passed away; behold, the new has come" (2 Corinthians 5:17 ESV).

Chapter 5

WHO IS GOD?

· ·

Katie May, mom of three, age thirty-three

When God began to stir in my life, I didn't know I was missing anything ... at all. I had attended Mass growing up, and I thought I had all I needed. Then something happened after my first daughter was born. I would stare at her and kiss her a million times a day and think about how wonderful she was and how blessed I was like any new mother. Also around this time, one of my sisters talked to me about Jesus, but I figured I was fine ... after all, I was Catholic, right?

One day as I sat there, enamored with my sweet girl, I felt something different, and all I could think about was Jesus. And that was it. I literally felt like He had answered my question for me, a question I didn't know I had. Out of nowhere, I sensed Him saying, "Me. You need Me." What I needed to do was turn my life over to Jesus and pass that gift on to my children. No other gift would ever matter.

So I guess my next step was figuring out what a relationship with Jesus meant. I had never heard of that in all my years of churchgoing, which is kind of sad now that I think about it. I could actually just talk to Him. I had so much regret at first for the life that I had led and the horrible things I had done to my body. If I was to be completely honest, I would say I was self-absorbed, reckless, and wild. I had settled down since meeting my husband and had grown up quite a bit, so I didn't go out and party like I used to, but I was still stuck with such a limited view of life. I just didn't get it. I cried so much that first year. Happy cries and sad cries.

Now I understand the freedom that comes with Jesus and the intimacy of the relationship God wants us to have with Him. I still get chills when I think about it. How He is right here, if I only seek Him. How He wants us to love Him, freely and openly. It makes me teary and humbles me daily. I can't even imagine the emptiness of my life before. I was so limited. I fail constantly at being a better person, but the amazing thing is that I can still try and I have a reason to, a hope. And I want to try. When I begin to stray from my prayer life, I can see it play out in everything that I do. When I don't constantly seek Him but seek only myself, I see the old me and I don't like it. So I start again. I didn't know that I could *love* Jesus. Now I get it ... and it is the best thing that's happened in my life.

The Bible says God "has planted eternity in the human heart" (Ecclesiastes 3:11 NLT). It makes sense then, that human beings have always been asking, "Who is God?" Scientists and archaeologists have been fascinated by this question, recently discovering that in earliest times people didn't gather to create religions and doctrines—rather they gathered to worship. Ancient civilizations were built around the desire to worship together.[1] Animals don't ask who God is

1   Charles C. Mann, "Göbekli Tepe: The Birth of Religion," *National Geographic*, June 2011, http://ngm.nationalgeographic.com/2011/06/gobekli-tepe/mann-text.

(unless they're an animal in one of Gary Larson's *The Far Side* comics), but human beings most certainly do.

There are two ways to look at this question, and the road we choose will make all the difference. God is either who *we* (human beings) say He is or who *He* says He is. And since there are many different views of religion, this question can get sticky. To discern who God is takes solid thinking and intellectual commitment because different religions describe God in different ways.

Some would like to avoid the intellectual rigor and just say all religions lead to the same place, employing a summary statement like, "That's all religion." However, nothing really works that way in life. It'd be like saying, "Take any road you want; they'll all end up at your house." We know it doesn't work that way. More aptly, it would be like saying all math equations will get you to the same result because, you know, "It's all math; it's all numbers." But if we said, "Would you like us to *add* five thousand dollars to your bank account or *subtract* five thousand dollars?" you'd say, "I want you to add five thousand dollars." If we then said, "Don't worry about it. What's the difference? It's just numbers; it's all math. It all ends up at the same place. Does it really matter?" you'd say,

"Yes, it matters. There's a big difference. And, yes, it's all math, but there's a big difference between addition and subtraction." Only a person who doesn't know much about math would say, "It doesn't matter if you add the numbers or subtract them—it's all just numbers."

It's the same way with religion. Most religions teach different things about how to get to God and about who God is. Only a person who doesn't know very much about religions would say that they're all the same and that they all lead to the same place.

Over the millennia, human beings have created many belief systems and religious ideas. Generally scholars make a distinction between a "belief system" and a "religion" through two core ingredients: a religion has a defined sense of a supreme being—a god figure—and a religion has a concept of an afterlife. From the Latin, the word *religion* means "to tie back together, to reconnect." That's helpful and at least gets us started with the idea that religion is to help us reconnect to God. But this assumes we got disconnected. Although other religions provide a path toward God, Christianity clearly understands that we are disconnected from God, and that God has offered us the way to be reconciled to Him through Jesus

Christ. So at this point it might be helpful to review what we've discussed as the main tenets of Christianity and how those differ from other religions.

Many religions teach that God is an otherworldly supreme being of some kind. They suggest that you and I would want to please this God if we want to have a good life and if we want to go to a better after-life when we die. But only one religion, Christianity, teaches that God has made that way for us because we are unable to do so ourselves. All other religions teach that we must make the way for ourselves by being good enough, doing enough good things, thinking the right things, doing the right religious practices, etc.[2]

Christianity is unique among religions because of the response to sin—our core character flaw that keeps us from God. While most religions try to answer the question of humankind's propensity toward selfishness and impurity, only Christianity teaches that God has provided the way (not *a* way, but *the* way) for our sins to be forgiven: through Jesus. We are unable to save ourselves, but Jesus can save us. This is possible because Jesus is unique—He is God's Son, fully God and fully man.

....

2   For an overview of religions and what they teach, *The World's Religions* by Huston Smith is a great resource.

Non-Christian religions teach that if we do the right things, practice the right religious practices, think the right things, etc., then perhaps we will be good enough. These religions have a core of "works" to them, a core of "human merit" to them—that we can be good enough for God if we … well, if we get religious enough and get it right. But the Bible says, "For all have sinned and fall short of the glory of God" (Romans 3:23), and we are not able to be good enough on our own. We cannot be good enough. That may offend you—and if it does, that is part of your journey. But the God we're talking about in this book, God the Creator of all that exists, God the Father of Jesus Christ, has informed us that we cannot have a relationship with Him except by receiving His offer of forgiveness through Jesus Christ (Galatians 3:22).

This is because God is perfect in every respect. And as we spoke about in chapter 3, our sin makes us different from God and separates us from Him. This also means we are unable to make ourselves perfect on our own, even if our "own" actions are works designed to bring us closer to God. Anything, any work that originates with us first could never be enough. We cannot use brokenness (our own work) to fix something broken (our own hearts) to get to something perfect (God). That's like trying to jump-start a dead car battery with another dead battery.

This is why God has offered Jesus Christ as a sacrifice for our sin—as a gift of forgiveness for us. This is what grace is about, and no other religion has it the same way. So now, understanding a few main things about God will help you as you begin to follow Him. Let's talk about four of God's characteristics and why they matter.

GOD IS ETERNAL

Have you ever tried to explain time to a child? Children live in time differently than adults do. Living in the moment, children have less of a grasp of the beginning and end of things and less of an understanding of the past and the future. A child of one of my (Nicole's) friends always referred to the future as "tomorrow." This child lived in constant expectation that his birthday, Christmas, and every other good thing was "tomorrow." Just as it's hard for a child to understand time, it's hard for any of us to understand eternity.

To say that God is eternal is to say that He never had a beginning. He is the one thing that has always existed. This is hard for us because everything we know, everything we have experienced or will experience (except heaven) has a beginning and an end. We simply have a hard time navigating the intellectual space that speaks about something, someone never actually having a beginning or an end.

We understand that things come from things. Trees come from seeds; children come from the union of their parents. Well enough, but this has to mean that there is a source. Something or someone is the progenitor of what comes next. This means that somewhere there had to be something that was always there, and this something is the source of all the other things. That something has to be "the initiator" of all the rest. That's true, but in our case it's not a some-thing we're talking about—it's a some-one. The Bible says, "There is but one God, the Father, *from whom all things came*" (1 Corinthians 8:6). This means He is the source and the progenitor of everything else.

We get big clues about God's eternal nature when God first introduced Himself to Israel's leader Moses by telling Moses that His name was I AM (Exodus 3:14). In the name "I AM," we notice both the present tense and the open-endedness (never endingness) of God. God introduced Himself to Moses as one who had no beginning and has no conclusion. God didn't say to Moses, "I was," or "I will be," nor did He say, "I was for a little while," or even, "I will be for a long while." No, I AM stands in the solitude of Himself. I AM stands beyond time as one who always is, always is alive, always is in the present tense.

The Bible begins with "in the beginning" but also makes it clear that God was there even before the beginning. Psalm 90:2 says, "From everlasting to everlasting you are God." Psalm 100:5 says, "The LORD is good and his love endures forever." In John 17:5 is the stunning statement that Jesus and God the Father were together before there ever was a created world: "Glorify me in your presence with the glory I had with you before the world began." Revelation 1:8 says, "'I am the Alpha and the Omega,' says the Lord God, 'who is, and who was, and who is to come, the Almighty.'" First Timothy 1:17 says He is the King, "eternal, immortal, invisible."

God uses every word there is to describe Himself as outside of time: *everlasting, eternal, forever, is, was,* and *is to come.* This is what we mean when we say God is eternal. Eternal doesn't mean a really, really long time. It means "timeless." It means "outside the dimension of time."

GOD IS RELATIONAL

The Bible teaches in many places that God exists as three persons together in perfect unity. This is called the Trinity. Just as it is difficult for us to grasp eternity, it's also difficult for us to grasp the Trinity, the three-person nature of God. Rather than being a solo God figure, the God of the Bible is God the Father, God the Son (Jesus Christ), and God the Holy Spirit. They are three distinct persons, but they live and work in perfect oneness. Hard to grasp, isn't it? For centuries, earnest people have tried to find ways to describe the Trinity. We find some three-in-one analogies in nature, for example. The sun doesn't exist without the light and the heat. All three are present. A person does not exist except with mind, emotion, and body. Time is past, present, and future. Yet all fall short of the picture God gives us of three persons living and working together in loving unity. Some actually find this to be a meaningful clue to the objective truth of this God—because He has revealed Himself in a way that is so unlike anything we human beings would have made up or been able to conceive from our own human-sized view of God.

Most religions have either a "one god" (solo god) concept (for instance, Islam and Judaism) or a "many gods" concept like Greek mythology or Hinduism.

The Christian faith is unique in the idea that God is one God, yet He is three persons: Father, Son, and Holy Spirit. The three live in perfect unity, which is why we speak of God's oneness. A solo God does not live in oneness; He lives alone. Oneness is a unity of more than one, where the unity is so complete that they live as one. We will all have eternity to plumb the depths and beauty of what this means.

The Bible has both implicit and explicit references to the Trinity. One explicit reference is found when Jesus was baptized. The Bible says not only that God was thrilled with Jesus but that all three members of the Trinity were present and active: "When all the people were being baptized, *Jesus* was baptized too. And as he was praying, heaven was opened and *the Holy Spirit* descended on him in bodily form like a dove. And *a voice came from heaven*: 'You are my Son, whom I love; with you I am well pleased'" (Luke 3:21–22). In this depiction, which appears also in the gospels of Matthew and Mark, we see *Jesus* being baptized, the *Holy Spirit* descending upon Him, and *God the Father* speaking from heaven. Another biblical reference where we see Jesus clearly talking about the Trinity is in Matthew 28:19. Here Jesus instructed His disciples to take the message of life in God to all nations and people. Note that He named all three members of the Trinity in this verse: "Therefore go and make disciples of all nations, baptizing them in the name of *the Father* and of *the Son* and of *the Holy Spirit*."

These sections and other implicit passages in the Bible reveal a dynamic relationship among the Father, the Son, and the Holy Spirit. In their relationship they are creating, redeeming, aiding, and intervening. They work together in ways that are harmonious and complementary, always in intimate relationship together, the three loving one another and working together in perfect unity. This has vast implications for us as human beings made in God's image.

Perhaps the most important implication is revealed in Genesis 1:26–28, where God said, "Let us make mankind in our image." Note the plural *us*. This means that God was speaking among the Trinity, and together They would create human beings. Further, if God has always lived in perfect relationship among the Trinity, and if we are made in His image, then we too are made for loving and intimate relationships. This means there is a longing in human hearts for intimacy that reaches for the deepest level of fulfillment.

Just this week in a staff meeting, one of our ministry leaders commented, "The fact that God exists in community expresses to us a picture of the greatest good." This relational God gives us a picture of how we participate in life together, sharing in one another's joys as well as challenges. Our hearts are truly designed for the dynamic of serving and loving that exists in the Trinity.

This is also why "being alone" is the first time anything is "not good" in the Bible. In the account of creation in Genesis 1, as God was creating things— land, sea, plants, and animals—we see a repetition of the statement "it was good."[3] But Genesis 2:18 stands in stark contrast to this statement. Adam was found alone, without a mate, and the Bible says, "It is not good for the man to be alone." Note that it was not Adam who said to God, "I'm lonely—can You do something about that?" No, it was God—who lives in the perfect love of the Trinity—who commented that Adam's solo status was "not good." And so God made Eve. The two are made to be complements to each other and to be helpers and completers for each other. So just as God has always lived in loving relationship among the Trinity, we, being made in God's image, are also made to be in loving and intimate relationship.

....

3   See Genesis 1:10, 12, 18, 21, 25.

GOD IS PERFECT

Recently, my wife and I (David) were having a conversation, and while we were talking about one topic (which is how men like to do it), Elisabeth brought up another topic (which is how women often do it). The first topic was about how I was trying to improve at something. Another thought came to mind for Elisabeth; and, well, being a woman, she can keep several thought streams going simultaneously. As I was talking about trying to improve, she said something like, "Maybe that's what you could give me for my birthday." Confused by this, I said, "What? You'd like me to give you improvement for your birthday?" This sparked some humor in the moment—which became a full-grown inside joke between us—"I was thinking I might give you universal improvement for your birthday. Yes, that's what I'll give you for your birthday—a much-improved version of myself."

This speaks to the tension we all feel inside to be better, and that's not a new concept. Martin Luther, a revolutionary church leader from the sixteenth century, said it this way: "This life therefore is not righteousness, but growth in righteousness, not health, but healing, not being but becoming…. We are not yet what we shall be." We all feel it: that yearning to be more than we are. This is another place where God is altogether different, because He is perfect.

God is not flawed and is never in need of improvement. This explains why God doesn't change—because to change would mean He is either getting better or getting worse. He's either improving or regressing. But a perfect God doesn't "get better," and He doesn't "get worse." That's part of being perfect.

How do we know God is perfect? Second Samuel 22:31 says, "His way is perfect: the LORD's word is flawless." Deuteronomy 32:4 says His "works are perfect." Matthew 5:48 says, "Your heavenly Father is perfect." Isaiah 25:1 says God exists in "perfect faithfulness." This word *perfect* means something like "complete in every way." This survey of the Bible explains that God is perfect in character, in the way He does things, in what He says, in how He works, and in what He wills. Additionally, the Bible makes it clear that since God is perfect, He is able to make things perfect through His own power. He is able to make things complete in every way. He is able to make us complete in every way. First Corinthians 13:12 says, "All that I know now is partial and incomplete [imperfect], but then I will know everything completely, just as God now knows me completely" (NLT). Wow. This perfect God knows you right now completely, perfectly—and when we join Him in eternity, we, too, will be complete, whole.

Being perfect means God is not lacking anything. He has no shortages—of character, purity, knowledge, power, or ability. Being complete, He is not maturing or going through personal growth, as though He were like us, needing to improve. He's not growing up, getting better, or evolving. Those things are needed only for people like us who are "not there yet," who need to grow or improve.

Especially in contrast to us, God is perfect morally. As we have noted, the Bible says, "God is light; in him there is no darkness at all" (1 John 1:5). His actions and His judgments are without moral blemish. His motives, too, are perfect. On the other hand, speaking again of us human beings, the Bible is clear that "all have sinned and fall short of the glory of God" (Romans 3:23). The "glory of God" in this case is His essence, the nature of His being. His perfect being. And we fall short of that.

To be morally perfect means that God cannot tolerate sin, as we discussed earlier. You might think this a weird concept, asking, "Isn't God able to do anything He wants? Why would He be so harsh as to not allow our imperfections in His presence?"

Perhaps it helps to use the analogy the Bible gives of light and darkness. Light, in its nature, cannot tolerate darkness. Darkness is obliterated in the presence of light, because the two natures cannot coexist. Just the mere presence of light … and darkness is no longer. Exodus 33 offers us a glimpse of this when God gave Moses the commandments he needed to lead God's people. When Moses asked to see God's glory, God said, "No one may see me and live" (Exodus 33:20). Later, we read that Moses was so close to God that his "face was radiant" (Exodus 34:30). His face emanated so much light after being close to the presence of God that he had to cover his face with a veil around people! God is light, and in Him is no darkness at all. He is morally perfect, and sin (darkness) is not part of who He is.

So, as light and darkness do not coexist, neither can the perfect God coexist with sin. This is good news, actually, because it means He is perfectly good; He's not a shady character who has under-the-table dealings like a mafia boss, as we mentioned previously. It means that all the sad, broken, hard, corrupt, violent things that are part of this world and our human hearts are not part of His. And one day, God will restore all things to the purity of His intended design (Revelation 21:4–5).

This is why we say that God is just. We, made in God's image, were born with this innate sense of justice. This is why parents all over the world have never had to teach their children to say, "That's not fair!" Kids just do. We are always rocked by injustice, whether it involves small things, like when someone cuts in line on the playground, or big things, like when crimes go unpunished. Deep within us, we have this sense of "that's not right!" *That's not right.* Where did we come up with that, unless something truly is not right and a moral repulsion in us is part of being made by the God who is perfectly just?

Most of us would agree that the thought of all things being made right, where injustices are addressed and where wrongs are dealt with, gives us hope. There's a reason why we joke about the standard Miss America answer: "I wish for world peace." World peace would come in a world that's fair and morally right. Where there was no wrongdoing, no tyrants, no sin. It's like the bumper sticker that says, "If you want peace, work for justice."[4] We long for this peace, and we know we have not—and perhaps never could in our own humanity—attained it. It's a longing we

. . . .

4   First said by Pope Paul VI and now found on bumper stickers everywhere.

all understand. It's a longing that comes because we were made in God's image, which means we have God-desires in us for eternal things, for perfect things, for just things.

GOD IS "OMNI"

When I (David) was a kid and an avid sports fan, a new sports arena called "the Omni" was built in Atlanta, Georgia. As a kid, I had no idea what the word *omni* meant. Only later did I learn that it means "all." When I learned that, it struck me as rather presumptuous for an arena to be named "all." Sounded kind of grandiose to me, or maybe a bit of a stretch. And back then I was not a person of faith, but I remember thinking it sounded as though the people who named it may have had some kind of a god complex since the word *all* seemed pretty comprehensive.

Much later, when I was in seminary, the *omni* word showed up again in force—especially in my first systematic theology class. It was there that I reencountered the word *omni*; it was used to describe God in three particular ways. He is *omnipresent*, He is *omnipotent*, and He is *omniscient*. These words mean (in order) that God is "all-present," that He is "all-powerful," and that He is "all-knowing." He is able to be everywhere simultaneously, He is powerful over all things, and He knows all things. That would make sense since God is "perfect," lacking nothing. So think about the word *all* for a minute, and it will help you grasp the bigness of God. "All things?" you might ask. Yes. All things. Nothing is excluded.

WHY IT MATTERS

There is a sense that in our everyday patterns of work, errands, and family, these big ideas of God don't really matter. A few weeks ago, I (Nicole) was doing some shopping with my husband, Dave. Excuse the stereotype, but I was very happy to be picking out new shirts and ties for Dave ... and he was, well, tolerant. As I browsed tie patterns, thoughts of God's omnipresence and perfectness were not at the front of my mind, or in my mind at all.

I heard the chimes of the store's door opening, and I looked up to see a high school student I know through our student ministry who lost his father earlier that year in an accident. Next came his mother, who is navigating raising children and running a business in a life she never expected or wanted, one where her husband is no longer with her. And in that one moment, an "everyday" moment, God's character mattered. Anything that feels unjust, anything that we cannot explain, anytime we are at a loss of understanding—God's character matters. Indeed, we received our own passion for justice from the God who made us—the passion that makes us protest to Him when we see something that feels unjust. Like a family losing a father.

As Dave and I left the clothing store that afternoon, understanding God mattered. Understanding God's eternity gives me hope. Knowing He's relational means I entered into a conversation with Him, asking Him to be with that family and to direct me into any words or actions that might be of comfort to that mother and son. Knowing God is perfect means that even when I do not understand, I can trust God. And knowing He is *all* means that He is the one who holds the power, that He has not left us alone, and that everything that is darkness and sadness and evil will be defeated. Eugene Peterson said it this way: "The fundamental fact of existence is that this trust in God, this faith, is the firm foundation under everything that makes life worth living. It's our handle on what we can't see" (Hebrews 11:1 MSG).

So who is God? He's the one who made you, He's the one who loves you beyond your wildest dreams, and He's the one who gave up His own Son, Jesus Christ, to death so He could have an eternal relationship with you. From the time He asked Adam, "Where are you?" He's been taking the first step and making the first move to restore our relationship with Him. He's the Creator of the cosmos, He never had a beginning, and He will never have an end. He is love; He is Spirit (rather than a bodily being); He is the Creator and giver of life. He is high and lifted up, outside of space and time … but He is also close—as close to you as your breath. If you'll let Him, He'll pour love into your soul that is sweeter than anything you've ever tasted. He'll remove your sins as far as the east is from the west, and He'll give you a new life—a new life forever, a new life that starts now.

So what happens when we know this God?

Knowing God changes our view of people—we start to see them as eternal souls, not temporary bodies.

Knowing God helps us face difficulties differently.

Knowing God means we never have to feel like life is out of control.

Knowing God grounds us in humility and purpose.

Knowing God helps life make sense.

Chapter 6

WHAT GOD WANTS
US TO KNOW

· ·

Rakesh Jain, cardiologist, age fifty-four

I was brought up in a relatively religious family;
my parents prayed every morning, and we regu-
larly went to the temple. We practiced Jainism, a
sect of Hinduism—thus my last name Jain. I was
almost twelve when we moved from India to
the United States—to Buffalo, New York, in the
middle of the winter. It was a huge change!

My first exposure to Jesus Christ occurred
shortly after we moved to the United States, as
my dad taught in a Catholic school in Buffalo. We
still practiced Jainism the best we could even
though there was no temple in town. Then I met

a woman named Diane, and we started dating. We got married in 1985. Religion was not a big issue for either of us in the first few years of marriage, but all of that changed after the birth of our first child.

Our initial plan was that we would teach our children equally about both of our religions and let them make up their minds as they grew older. But it didn't take long for us to realize this wasn't smart or practical unless we wanted to raise some confused kids. Although I agreed in principle to let Diane raise the kids in the Christian church, it bothered me to think of how disappointed my family would be that I allowed such a thing.

And I wasn't just not Christian; I was anti-Christian. My relationship with Diane went through a difficult time. Even though I was vocally against this faith, deep down, I was uncomfortable with my stance. I knew I wasn't practicing any faith, so I would question myself about why I was so upset that Diane and the kids had faith, even if it was different from what I believed.

While I struggled with this issue, I came into contact with a lot of Christian people both socially and professionally—which I don't think, looking back, was an accident. As a doctor, I must have had more than twenty pastors and missionaries within my practice. I admired them. The way they lived grew my interest in Christianity. I would say that all of the people who had a positive impact on me had one thing in common: they were followers of Christ. These people met me where I was and started a friendship without having a specific agenda. My spiritual growth was in some ways a by-product of those relationships.

While this was going on, I had some health issues and ended up needing major heart surgery. I began to reflect on what was truly important and pondered what would happen if I died in surgery. With the possibility of death becoming real, I had to look deeper and see if Christianity was for me. I found myself drawn to the one thing unique to believers in Christ: the resurrection. I also liked the concept of this relationship being a gift and not something that you can buy or earn.

My relationship with God now is very honest, and I try to live each day to the best of my abilities, thinking all the time about how Christ would have me act. I have my shortcomings, and most days I stray, but I ask God for His forgiveness and try to build on it. With Christ, I find life richer and more meaningful in almost every way.

Some of us are born with a sense of direction, and some of us are instinctually deficient. I (Nicole) fall into the latter category. My colossal lack of direction manifests itself on a daily basis. When I come out of a store at the mall, I usually end up walking back in the direction from which I just came. I get lost running through my own neighborhood. Once I drove an hour in the wrong direction on the way home from a retreat—until the "Welcome to Georgia" sign on I-95 alerted me that we were, in fact, not heading north toward Virginia. And, as my husband likes to point out, I have the double malady of no directional sense coupled with the confidence that I'm right, even when I'm wrong. That combination is what gets me driving down a highway sixty miles in the wrong direction without even realizing there's a problem.

Life can be a little like this as well. We can be just a few degrees off course, and over the long run we end up very far from our original direction.

Beginning a relationship with God is the ultimate course correction. It doesn't matter how far off course you've gone; at some point you realize you aren't sure where you are and you aren't sure where you are going. Jesus Christ introduces you to your starting point (where you are right now) and your ending, or eternal point (life forever with Him). But life can be a winding maze of different footpaths and highways. To make it more complicated, where you are might not be where anyone else around you is right now. You might be a college student reading this in your dorm room, a man who is out of work, a stay-at-home mom who hadn't thought about Jesus since Sunday school as a kid, or a doctor who's felt God stirring for the first time. We all find our "start here" at different places on the journey.

We don't know the exact circumstances of where you are starting, but the good news is that God does. And because He is perfect, as we discussed in the last chapter, He has picked the right time to come into your life. And because He's the Creator and designer of the human heart, this starting point makes sense for you.

STAYING THE COURSE

If you have begun a relationship with Jesus by giving Him the truth of yourself—asking Him to forgive

you and receiving Him as the Lord of your life—
you're a new believer in Christ. A new person in
Christ. We talked in chapters 3 and 4 about receiving
Jesus and the gifts He gives us—new eternity, new
identity, new family, new character. By accepting
His gift, you've begun a transparent and honest relationship with Jesus Christ. Now that you're on that
course, focused on Jesus, don't stray from it.

In the future you will (or perhaps you already
have) come across a lot of different things that people
are going to tell you about Christianity. Most of
them will come from people who seem like "super
Christians." Super Christians will tell you that
Christianity is "Jesus and …" Jesus and this thing or
that, this theological idea or that, this spiritual experience or that, this way of behaving or that. Most of
these are ways that people try to convince themselves
or other people—or perhaps God—that they are
super Christians. There are a million reasons why our
hearts might be inclined in this direction—to prove
that we belong, that we are worthy, that we are special,
that we are powerful. These are all efforts one way or
another to try to assuage our insecurities. As if being
a son or daughter of God wasn't enough, some people
will suggest that you need "extra touches."

Unfortunately, this super Christianity usually ends up being a religion show—outward appearances engineered to impress. Jesus, fully God and fully understanding our hearts, made it clear that this religion show is a real temptation for us—a way for us to feel better about ourselves while avoiding a real relationship with Him (John 5:39–44). In the gospel of John, Jesus called out the "super religious" Jewish leaders for this very thing, telling them, "You study the Scriptures diligently because you think that in them you have eternal life … yet you refuse to come to me" (John 5:39–40). From beginning to end, *Start Here* is talking about the process of coming to Him—coming to Jesus honestly, receiving the gift of His forgiveness, and entering into a lifelong journey with your Father God. This journey is not, and never will be, about following rules or about doing things "right." Rather, this is about an everyday relationship with Jesus Christ that is honest and transparent.

God teaches us that Christianity is a relationship. His promises are "I will take you as my own people, and I will be your God" (Exodus 6:7) and "I am with you always, to the very end of the age" (Matthew 28:20). These statements make it clear that our life with God is a relationship, and it is lived out like all long-lasting relationships. Because God has made it clear that this is what it's about, relationship is the best way we can understand how life with God actually happens. Will you be changed by this relationship? Yes, of course. Any significant and committed relationship will change most everything about the way you live your life. But the relationship comes first, and those changes come as we journey and live and love together. This is the essential core of our relationship with Christ.

We also say this to make the distinction from other ways people talk about Christianity or describe Christians. Sometimes people may say things like, "Wow, you've gotten religious," which tends to impose pressure that now you must make yourself a better person. Ideas like those are knockoff versions of Christianity: counterfeit currencies that have the appearance of religion but no real value. They tempt us toward an outward show that over time produces no real life change, no joy. The real version of Christianity as described in the Bible is a living relationship with Jesus Christ as we walk with Him and follow Him each day—a relationship where He is present with us at all times and in all circumstances, whether happy or hard.

Like in all relationships, we grow and learn as we seek to love and be faithful. *If* we seek to love and be faithful. All relationships have seasons and ups and downs. This is normal, and it will be normal in our life with God. The key is that we continue to seek not "to master" Him, but *to be with Him*. We cannot overemphasize the importance of this point as you begin your relationship with God.

So to reiterate once again, *Christianity is not a religious formula*. Formulaic thinking shrinks the beauty and the wonder of God. You may think, *Of course God's not a formula!* But these views creep up on us gradually, and that's why we want to address them now. Such formulas are false versions of the real God. Here are a few examples.

THE "MAKE ME HAPPY" GOD

Over time, many people fall into a version of Christianity that believes, without saying it, that God is supposed to make our lives go well. We see it as His job. We have a picture of what we want our lives to be, and we fall into a rut of believing that God's job is to make our pictures become reality. This is absolutely not the biblical picture of life with God, but a cheap version, a fake copy grown out of our self-centeredness. Here's a progression of how this version usually develops:

God saved me and offers me life
and forgiveness.

This must mean that God wants
my life to be happy and go the
way I envision it.

If hard things happen to me, this
makes me question if God is
reliable.

If my life picture is not coming
true, it must mean that either
God is punishing me or He is
not who I thought He was.

If a tragedy happens in my life, it
must mean that God is either
incapable or unloving. Either He
was not capable of stopping it—
which means I now have a crisis
of faith—or He doesn't love me
(or is punishing me or cursing
me), which gives me a crisis of
heart.

Ultimately, without knowing it, this form of
belief means that *my* picture of *my* life is the highest
object of my devotion and that God is supposed to

serve me and make my picture come true. This is the core formula that drives the beliefs and crises of belief for many thousands of people who thought they were living a Christian life. This version of Christianity is, first, not Christianity at all. It is like comparing a well-crafted, robust, and complex cabernet sauvignon to a Hi-C juice box. The two may look somewhat the same and be derived from the same fruit (or "artificial fruit flavor"), but there is no comparison. This prosperity idea of Christianity is a poor substitute that is unbiblical and will not hold up to life's realities and challenges (Isaiah 53; John 16:33; Philippians 3:10; Luke 9:23).

THE IF-THEN GOD

Another formula of unspoken and sometimes invisible beliefs is the "if-then" formula:

> *If* I am good, *then* God should reward me.
>
> *If* I do the right thing and make the choice of integrity, *then* God must make things go well.
>
> *If* I'm a good spouse, *then* God must make my marriage happy.

If I do the right things as a parent,
    then God must give me happy,
    accomplished children.

These examples and others like them are the
false beliefs that come with formulaic Christianity. In
its full expression, this is not what the Bible teaches
about Christianity. We should reemphasize that the
Bible makes clear that we will face both the pleasant
and the painful in life. Both were part of Jesus's life
on earth, and since it was true for Jesus—God's own
Son—it will be true for us. Jesus said as much: "In
this world you will have trouble. But take heart! I have
overcome the world" (John 16:33). Furthermore, God
does much of His most meaningful work in our lives
through difficult circumstances. It is often in times of
loneliness, in hardship, and in all manners of trouble
when we find that we grow the most.

So life with God is not a math formula; it's a love
story where God's heart says to yours, "I love you; I
died for you; I will be with you in every breath of your
life, through the joys and the tragedies." The apostle
Paul said it this way: "I want to know Christ—yes,
to know the power of his resurrection and participation in his sufferings" (Philippians 3:10). Your life

experiences will offer you ample opportunity to know Christ—sharing in the happy and hard, the joyful and the painful, the resurrection victory, and the suffering of a broken world.

Okay, so the point that we hope you've gotten loud and clear by now is that Christianity is not something to accomplish—it's not a rule book, and it's not a performance or formula. It's an intimate and growing relationship with Jesus Christ. Christianity is a daily, interactive relationship with Jesus, where I am giving my life to Him and He is giving His life to me.

KEEPING IT NATURAL

Years ago I (David) was traveling through Asia to visit with Christian leaders. My trip began in New Zealand and Australia, where I was meeting with some Christians who are active in supporting ministries in the Asia-Pacific region. Since this was my first time in these countries, I was pumped to experience all the newness and hear the Aussie accents. (Not sure why Aussie accents sound so cool to us Americans, but they do. I can't imagine that our accents sound cool to them.) One afternoon I was on a ferry, touring some islands off the coast of New Zealand with a few other men. One was a friend who worked with a ministry based in the States, and the other was a Kiwi businessman named Ken, who was involved with a Bible-teaching ministry. That afternoon, with the sun shining and a warm breeze over the water, Ken and I talked about our faith in Jesus. He said, "David, I remember when I was a teenager and I was asking an older man about the best way to live out my faith. I was asking him how to share Jesus with other people and how to grow as a Christian. After I talked and he listened for a while, the elderly man turned and said to me, 'Ken, the secret is to *let your spiritual life be natural and let your natural life be spiritual.*' And I've never forgotten it."

Well, from the moment Ken said that to me, I, too, have never forgotten it. In a warm interaction with this new friend, as I looked at the beauty of the New Zealand coastline on a sunny afternoon, that conversation lodged in my memory. That sentence has become an anchor statement in my understanding of living the Christian life. *Let your spiritual life be natural, and let your natural life be spiritual.*

So by now you can tell it's our desire to help you experience the joy of daily, natural life with Jesus Christ. But more than *our* desire to help you know this is *God's* desire that you would know this, which is one reason He provides tangible ways for us to experience some of His greatest promises. The big religious word for this is *sacraments*.

You might read that word and think, *Sacraments? Whoa, that doesn't sound very natural.* We understand, but with a little learning we can begin to see how sacraments are both spiritual and natural. The sacraments are the building blocks for the way God wants us to experience life with Him and to be reassured of all that He offers us.

OUTWARD AND VISIBLE SIGNS ...

First, a definition of the word *sacrament*. There are many, but we'll use a simple one from Augustine of Hippo: a sacrament is "a visible sign of an invisible reality." Having visible signs of invisible things is very helpful to us in life—and in Christian life in particular. This is because we are people who are used to living in the physical world around us. We see, touch, hear, and taste things that are physical and tangible. But the Bible says, "God is spirit" (John 4:24), which means we can't touch Him in the same physical way. We can't see Him or understand Him in the same ways we understand many other things. God knows this about us, and this is one reason He's given us sacraments. These help us understand God, what He's done for us, and how to live in Him. So the sacraments are a gift to us—to help us see and know and understand. Throughout church history, different schools of thought have developed about what a real sacrament is. But for our purposes, we will limit our use of this word to the two acts that Jesus demonstrated in the New Testament: baptism and Communion.

BAPTISM

Baptism is the sacrament that marks the beginning of life in a relationship with Jesus Christ. Generally speaking, a person is baptized once, and it is a mark of his or her beginnings in God. (This is different from Communion, which is an ongoing and repeated practice for Christians.) Over the centuries, Christians have come to two main views of baptism: infant baptism and believer's baptism. For the sake of *Start Here*, we'll briefly describe the two, but we don't intend to go deeper than that. You can read and research this on your own if you'd like.

Infant baptism is when a very young child is brought for baptism by his or her Christian parents. When an infant is baptized, he or she is not actively engaged in the process. Part of the unspoken message of this is the acknowledgment that God works in our lives long before we ever know it. It marks the promise that God is making through Jesus Christ, that forgiveness of sin and new life are offered. And even though the child doesn't understand yet what's happening, God is still offering. He has a very active role. In other words, God was inviting you long before you realized it. The sign of this offer of forgiveness and new life in Jesus is water sprinkled or poured over the child's head.

Believer's baptism is slightly different. This is when a person has come to a place where he or she understands God's offer of life in Jesus and is being baptized as an expression that he or she has accepted this offer. Believer's baptism emphasizes that the person being baptized has made a conscious decision to receive Jesus as Lord and Savior. In believer's baptism, a person may be momentarily immersed under water, which symbolizes that this person has died to self and is raised to new life in Jesus.

While infant baptism and believer's baptism are both about life in Jesus, infant baptism puts emphasis on God making the offer while believer's baptism emphasizes the person saying yes to God's offer. Either way, one of the powerful aspects of this sacrament is that someone else carries out your baptism. This signifies a relational participation with other believers (the church) as an integral part of your life in Christ. Part of what's being conveyed, since you can't baptize yourself, is that we do this life of faith together.

There's more to baptism, of course (approximately one million books more), but we're interested in fostering unity rather than debating. And since that's the case, we're going to talk about the core idea of baptism—mainly that when we receive Jesus Christ, God washes us clean from sin and adopts us into His family. Water marks the washing, since water is the universal agent for cleansing. And not only are we washed, but we are also cleansed of all unrighteousness. The Bible goes further, making it clear that Jesus takes our sin *and* our shame (Genesis 3:21; Isaiah 61:10; Romans 10:9–11; 1 Peter 2:24). So baptism is a sign that God forgives us, cleanses us from sin, and takes our guilt and shame. Indeed, God in His grace and love has been covering our guilt and shame from the very earliest time of sin.

Remarkably, the Bible repeatedly speaks of God not only cleansing us but also covering us. He did this in Genesis—covering Adam and Eve with clothing when they rejected Him—and thereafter the Bible repeatedly connects our forgiveness with "being clothed." How kind of God not only to accept us, not only to cleanse us, but also to clothe us in garments of grace, to cover our shame (Isaiah 61:10; Luke 15:22). All of these things show how God gives us a new start with a clean record, and if you've lived some life and experienced the pain and shame of regret, a new start with a clean record is an awesome gift.

Dying and Living

Entering this place of being forgiven comes when we accept Jesus Christ, expressing, "I want to accept the offer of Jesus's forgiveness and new life."

With this, we are saying, "I am surrendering myself as the center of my life and inviting Jesus Christ to be the center of my life."

Or again, saying to God, "I want to stop living my way for me; I want to start living Your way for You."

Sometimes you hear this referred to as "dying to self" (see Romans 6:2; 2 Corinthians 5:15). Becoming a Christian for real means I've come to a place where I no longer want to live for myself, but I want to live for God. So I'm "dying to me and living to Him."

This story of a military chaplain illustrates the concept of laying ourselves down when we repent and receive Jesus. The chaplain, deployed for Operation

Desert Storm, had many soldiers come to him to receive baptism and declare their new standing in Christ. When he began to search for a receptacle to hold water for baptism, the chaplain realized that coffins were all they had. And so a coffin was lined with a body bag, then filled with water … and those who wished were baptized in the coffin—giving each one an even more illustrative experience of lying down in the water in the coffin and then being raised from it. What better symbol of dying to self and being raised to new life in Christ?[1]

Yes, baptism marks God's offer of salvation and the beginnings of new life in relationship with Jesus Christ. It illustrates and teaches us about the incredible gift of cleansing and forgiveness that Jesus Christ offers when we die to ourselves and receive Him. You may think this idea of "dying to self" (see Matthew 16:25) sounds frightening—and we fully understand. It scared me (David) when I first heard it. Remarkably, however, people have shared again and again throughout Christian history that this is when they began to feel fully alive for the first time—finally feeling free, feeling like themselves! One of our favorite experiences

....

1   Ken Hemphill, *We Are (Kingdom Promises)* (Nashville: B&H Books, 2006), 57.

in ministry is being part of baptism services. It's meaningful for everyone involved—the new believer, the leaders, and the community. If you've begun a relationship with Jesus and you've never been baptized, we encourage you to take that step. It'll be an important mark in your own history, a tangible reminder of your new life with Christ.

COMMUNION

We have repeatedly emphasized in this book that God is a relational God. (We trust you've gotten that point by now!) This is seen throughout the Bible. As we mentioned before, in the Old Testament, the phrase (or one very similar to it) "I will be your God, and you will be My people" appears in numerous places (Genesis 17:7; Exodus 6:7; Leviticus 26:12; Jeremiah 30:22; and many others). This is a distinctly relational phrase that speaks of a lasting relationship with the God who makes and keeps His promises.

Traditionally, the making of a promise as the foundation of a relationship is called a covenant. A covenant is an expression of commitment and faithfulness. We think of this most often in regard to a "marriage covenant." But a marriage covenant is not something we human beings made up—it's something we have learned from God. The Bible speaks of God as a God who makes and keeps His covenant of faithful love for His people (Genesis 17:2–7). God clarified this idea of covenant through a man named Abraham, the first person in the Bible described as someone who "trusted God." This trust, this faith, was the core of his relationship with God and the reason God chose Abraham to be the father of the faith. And, to mark the depth and meaning of this relationship, God demonstrated His intentions of faithfulness through a ceremony called a "blood covenant."[2]

This ceremony was generally practiced between two people who intended to enter into a relationship of trust. It was marked by the sacrifice of an animal that was bilaterally cut in two (lengthwise) and laid on the ground (we know, sounds weird, but this was about four thousand years ago). When this animal was sacrificed, the two parties participating in the covenant would walk through the middle of the two halves of the animal. In doing this, walking through the spilled blood, they expressed to each other, "May what happened to this animal happen to me if I should break this covenant." Furthermore, in passing between the two halves, the two participants symbolically "took

....

2   Find the whole story in Genesis chapters 12–15.

each other's place" as a mark of their complete intentions to enter into the trust relationship. This action stated, "I will be in your place, and you will be in mine." At that time, a time before laws and police officers and jails, a covenant was the strongest expression of a promise that two parties could make to each other.

Turn the clock ahead approximately two thousand years to Jesus meeting with His disciples at what is traditionally called "the Last Supper." This meal was actually the Jewish Passover, a remembrance meal that Jews celebrate yearly. Think of this as similar to our Thanksgiving holiday. Passover marked God's liberation of the Jewish people from slavery in Egypt. It was rooted in the history of God's covenant relationship with His people. Keep in mind that at this "last supper," Jesus's disciples were Jewish men who were aware of the Jewish history—and what a covenant was. They knew about the covenant with Abraham and knew God freed the Jews from their Egyptian captivity.

At the meal, Jesus took bread, and after giving thanks, He broke it, saying, "This is my body given for you" (Luke 22:19; see also Matthew 26:26; Mark 14:22). When He said this, His disciples would have traced His words to the idea of the animal that was sacrificed in a covenant ceremony: the body being "broken."

Jesus went on to say, "As often as you eat of it, remember what I have done for you." In that moment, the disciples may well have understood that Jesus was saying that His body would be sacrificed. Furthermore, the disciples would have remembered Jesus giving them words of comfort when He said, "I am the way and the truth and the life. No one comes to the Father except *through* me" (John 14:6). Yes, the idea of coming to God "through" Jesus was very much like the covenant ceremony of walking "through" the two halves of a sacrificed animal. And Jesus was also suggesting to the disciples that by this covenant, as in that ancient covenant practice, they would "exchange places"; He would take their place (of sin), and they would be given His place of honor.

Upon hearing His words, they would begin to understand that Jesus was the final sacrifice, the new covenant sacrifice from God, the One through whom they—and all people—might come to God. In this moment at the Passover meal, Jesus made it clear that He was the sacrifice that would usher in a new covenant, a new promise, and the final sacrifice for all time.

In the breaking of bread at Communion, God wants us to know and trust that Jesus is the final sacrifice for us and the One through whom we come to God. This same promise carries over to the way Jesus also instructed His disciples with the "cup" in the Communion sacrament.

After breaking the bread, Jesus held up the cup of wine at the meal and said, "This cup is the new covenant in my blood, which is poured out for you" (Luke 22:20) … "do this, whenever you drink it, in remembrance of me" (1 Corinthians 11:25). Jesus was teaching them that when they drank this wine as an expression of a sincere faith in receiving Him, they were—in a spiritual expression—ingesting the blood He shed.

So where does the wine go next? Down the throat and into the stomach before being disseminated through the bloodstream. In a sense, the blood of the Son of God is in us. What a powerful spiritual truth! It means that God wants us to understand that we are His children, so much so that now we actually (spiritually) have the family blood in us. That's exactly what He wants us to believe. God wants us to be reminded every time we take Communion (i.e., receive Jesus) that through Jesus's sacrifice, we have been adopted by God—we've become His children.

So this clarifies that we are *truly* His children? Yes. We are truly His children.

So the sacraments, which to some sound like big religion words, are actually very earthy. Quite organic. Very relational. Deep with theological meaning. The sacraments are God's gift to us so we may know that through Jesus

- we are fully forgiven,
- we are given new life,
- we have really become children of God, and
- we can live freely in this new life He's given us.

If the meaning of this is sinking in for you, it may elicit the same feelings for you that it does for us. It may make you want to shout, "God, thank You so much!"

Chapter 7

GROWING *IN*

· ·

Hunter Glotz, student, age seventeen

It was a little bit weird when I was first picking up on the idea of going to church and becoming a Christian. I remember knowing and acknowledging that God was real, but I was so opposed to it. I can play it back in my mind like a film—just standing in the fourth row on the right side of the church, next to my friend who kept dragging me there, my arms crossed, a blank expression on my face. I felt uncomfortable singing out to a God I thought I didn't believe in. I think I mostly felt uncomfortable and worried that no one would accept me. I wanted to lock every door of my personal life. What would these church kids think of me after the things I'd done? I didn't know anything about the Bible! I didn't know that there were *two* testaments! I didn't know that Christians recognized the fact that they were imperfect.

About two months later, Jesus brought a wrecking ball to my life, and my walls fell in. I could sense it. It felt like God was doing this, and it felt right. I can't imagine the way my friend who brought me to church felt when he saw me now worshipping God. He said something along the lines of, "See! This is what I wanted you to understand."

From that point on, I had no idea what God what was doing in me, but I was changing. There was a point when the same friend who led me to God told me, "I remember you used to cuss all the time, and now you've stopped." This is when I knew God was working inside of me. I hadn't planned to stop using bad language all the time, but it just happened. If I had it my way, I probably would not have even changed, but it seems God had something He wanted to change in me.

I would like to think that I am a completely different person than I was five years ago. I think the only thing God didn't throw away was my ability to play music. Now I use that to help lead worship. I was a vagabond; now I am adopted. I was so lost and I had so many flaws, but Jesus already took that on the cross. God always loved me. I finally love Him back. I really see God putting me in situations with people who are just like I was before I became a Christian. I love sharing my story! Although I wish I hadn't done a lot of things, I love being the person who didn't grow up in church—the one who made this choice without it being forced upon him.

I wish my relationship with Christ was perfect, but it's not. It's up and down. All the ups come from God, and all the downs come from me. That's something I didn't know would happen when I accepted Christ. I thought everything would be okay, but it's clear in the Bible that we all fall short of the glory of God. Yet God stays true to us if we ask Him to come in.

A relationship is something you are *in*. Think about it—even Facebook gives you the public opportunity to proclaim you are "in a relationship." Obvious? Maybe,

but there's more to it than that. Think of other prepo-
sitions that don't work here, like, "on a relationship,"
"at a relationship," "with a relationship"—no, none
of these words work. You are *in* a relationship. It's
something you enter. The Bible says it the same way
repeatedly when describing Christianity. Just two of
many examples are "Therefore, if anyone is *in* Christ,
the new creation has come: The old has gone, the new
is here!" (2 Corinthians 5:17), and "When I am raised
to life again, you will know that I am in my Father,
and you are in me, and I am in you" (John 14:20 NLT).
Yet again, we're reminded that Christianity is not so
much something you believe but a relationship you
enter.

This concept that Christianity is a full relational
experience was shown in a meaningful way when Jesus
had a conversation with a woman named Martha,
which we mentioned in chapter 1. Jesus said to her, "I
am the resurrection and the life. The one who believes
[*into*] me will live, even though they die; and whoever
lives by believing [*into*] me will never die. Do you
believe this?" (John 11:25–26).[1]

. . . .

1   The use of the word *into* is based on the Greek word *eis*, which
     means "into." See *Novum Testamentum Graece: Nestle-Aland
     (Greek Edition)*, 26th Edition (1983).

Jesus had a similar conversation with Peter the disciple. Peter declared that he believed Jesus is the Savior and said: "We have *entered into* a state of belief and knowledge"[2] that "you are the Holy One of God" (John 6:69).

Did you catch the word *into* as "whoever believes *into* me will never die" and "we have entered *into* a state of belief"? "Believe *into*?" you might ask. "What does that mean?" This is what real belief does; it brings us to a place where we "enter" something—a relationship or an experience or a belief that changes us.

For example, if you believe (trust) that the cable on a zip line will hold you, you will then act on that trust and "enter into the belief" by jumping from the platform—thereby entering the zip-line experience. In order, you believe-trust-act-enter.

As a woman, if you believe in the character and affection of a man whom you have grown to love deeply (i.e., you trust him), then when he asks you to marry him, you act on your trust and "enter into the marriage relationship" by saying yes to his marriage proposal. See it? You believe-trust-act-enter.

....

2   See *The NIV Study Bible* (Grand Rapids: Zondervan, 2011) note on John 6:69 regarding the use of the Greek perfect tense, meaning "we have entered into and now are in" a state of belief.

In the case of the zip line, you "entered into the zip-line experience" when you took action and jumped from the platform. In the case of the marriage proposal, because you love and trust the man who asked you to marry him, you "entered into the marriage" (even though the wedding is still months away) by saying yes to the proposal. And in the case of Jesus Christ, when you come to believe, come to trust Him, you respond by saying yes to Him. You enter into this relationship.

Remember John 1:12: "To all who did receive him, to those who believed in his name, he gave the right to become children of God." Receiving Him is how you begin this relationship. It's the beginning of a never-ending adventure of continuing to receive Him in all experiences of life. John spoke of "believing in His name," which is the same idea of trusting Him we've been talking about. Upon trusting Him (trusting who He is and trusting His character), we enter into a committed relationship with Him.

This concept is further enhanced when we dig deeper into the Bible's word for *believe*. In the New Testament's original language (Greek), the word for *believe* is much fuller than our English word. It incorporates both belief and trust. A more accurate way to understand the word would be to combine *believe* and *trust* into one word, so John 3:16 would read, "For God so loved the world that he gave his one and only Son, that whoever *believes-trusts* in him shall not perish but have everlasting life." Here we are again, with the "belief-trust" that is the premise of entering a committed relationship. This is the "believe-trust-act-enter" of life with Christ.

So we now see that being a Christian involves much more than believing something in your head. We act upon belief and trust as we "enter into" a relationship with Jesus. Yes, we believe *into* Him. And believing into Him brings some new ways of life.

THE POWER OF *IN*

Now that we have established that being a Christian is about "being in" Jesus, we come to the question of "what's next?" You might be thinking, *Okay, I get it. I believe into Jesus and have received Him. Now what do I do? Where do I go next? How do I grow in this relationship?*

Put most plainly, you begin a life of "abiding" in Him and "remaining" in Him.[3] What does that mean? It means you seek to grow into your relationship with

....

3   For a full understanding of this idea, read John 15.

Him by bringing your heart, soul, mind, and strength (strength refers to your commitment and your will) fully into the relationship (Mark 12:30; Luke 10:27). You have begun with Him; now you grow by being *in* Him and seeking Him and leaning into Him in all experiences of life. But what we want to reiterate is that even though you grow in Him, this doesn't mean there is an arrival point. We will remain and grow in Him every day of our lives. There is never a time when we will master this relationship with Jesus, just as there is never a time when we will master a marriage. This doesn't always come easily. Our friend Jenn said it this way: "I can remember being an anxious person about small details in my life, and someone told me to 'rest and lay back in Jesus.' I was a little frustrated at this response because it felt so powerless. I wanted a step-by-step instruction manual on the things I could do while laying back and resting in Jesus!"

This is a part of how Jenn grew, and it may be a part of how you grow. Abiding or resting can take real discipline and trust.

To more fully illustrate the idea of remaining or "laying back in Jesus," Jesus Himself said it this way: "Remain in me, as I also remain in you. No branch can bear fruit by itself; it must remain in the vine.

Neither can you bear fruit unless you remain in me. I am the vine; you are the branches. If you remain in me and I in you, you will bear much fruit; apart from me you can do nothing" (John 15:4–5).

Do you know that all living things live *in* something? Trees and bushes and flowers live and thrive *in* the ground. Fish live and thrive *in* the water. Beautifully, we see this order in Genesis 1 when God created. He said, "Let the land produce vegetation" (Genesis 1:11), and "Let the water teem with living creatures" (Genesis 1:20). Reading this, you begin to understand that the first element (land or water) is the source of life for its living things. The land is the source of life for the trees and vegetation. The water is the source of life for the fish. If you remove a fish from the water, it will soon die. If you uproot a tree from the ground, it will soon die.

Then we come to the place of *in* for human beings: "So God created mankind in his own image, in the image of God he created them; male and female he created them" (Genesis 1:27). There is much to be said about this passage, which is one of the most significant verses in the Bible. But for our purposes, we'll stick with the idea of living things and their source of life. The land yields the vegetation, the water yields the fish, and now we see that God created human beings. And, continuing on the theme, this means that a person is alive as God intended when *in* relationship with God in a similar way that a tree is alive when rooted *in* the ground and a fish is alive when immersed *in* the water. The New Testament says it this way: "In [God] we live and move and have our being" (Acts 17:28). Sounds exactly like a fish living and moving and having its being in water, doesn't it? The fish out of water soon dies. Similarly, we see in the Bible that as human beings, to be alive is to be in a relationship with God—the One who made us and breathes life into us.

You may be thinking, *Maybe, but there are lots of people who are alive and well and not in a relationship with God.* True. But when we say "alive," we mean this in the entire spiritual sense, not just the physical. We're talking about being fully alive with "God life." Remember, we've talked before about the idea that we are beings with souls—and how that goes against what the world generally thinks about humanity. So, if you keep in mind that we are eternal beings with souls, the idea of being dead without God holds up. Our souls, that deepest part of us, live only when we are in God. This is the "reborn" aspect of Christianity. Through Christ, God gives us the opportunity for this new life—with a clean slate, a soul now alive, a new way of living … a rebirth. Hence why we say that *to be alive is to be in a relationship with God.*

In addition to every created thing having its place to be *in*, we observe the truth that every created thing also has a place to belong. Never once do we hear dogs bemoaning the fact that they are not cats. Never once do we see trees pulling themselves up by their roots and moving because they don't like their neighbors or their view. Human beings are the only creatures who struggle to find their place to belong. Perhaps it's true, as Augustine said, that "our hearts are restless until they rest in Thee."[4] And yes, we may not see people immediately go "belly up" like a fish out of water when they are not *in* God. But we will find that people remain restless at the deepest level, searching for a place to belong. And it is only in a relationship with Christ that our hearts are most alive and settled. In the fullest sense, being in Christ means we have come home where we belong.

So if a tree is to live and grow, it will do so deeply rooted into the ground. If a fish is to live and grow, it will do so immersed in the water. And now we've

....

4   Augustine, *Confessions* (Indianapolis: Hackett Publishing, 2006), 3.

learned that if we want to live and grow, this happens when we are rooted and immersed in our relationship with God. Yes, Jesus said it: "Remain in me and I [will remain] in you" (John 15:5).

So as we go through this last chapter of *Start Here*, we want to offer some guidance for how we stay "in relationship" with Jesus Christ. Here are five ways:

- In relationships with other Christians
- In God's guidance by reading and learning the Bible
- In conversation with God, through prayer
- In taking action through serving
- In expressing love for God through worship

IN RELATIONSHIPS: THE CHURCH

Many towns are full of pretty churches. But actually, they are full of pretty church buildings, because biblically speaking, the church is *people*. If you had some background in the church as a child, this translation of the church from a building to people can be made more difficult because of something you may have been taught. Ready? Put your hands together: "Here's the church, here's the steeple, open the doors, and see all the people." That's a nice rhyme, but it's horrible teaching on the church. At our church we say, "Friends don't let friends teach this to their kids!" No, the church is people, and one of the best general descriptions of the church comes from 1 Corinthians 1:2, where the apostle Paul said, "To the church of God in Corinth, to those sanctified in Christ Jesus and called to be his holy people, together with all those everywhere who call on the name of our Lord Jesus Christ—their Lord and ours."

In more everyday language, *The Message* says it this way: "I send this letter to you in God's church at Corinth, believers cleaned up by Jesus and set apart for a God-filled life. I include in my greeting all who call out to Jesus, wherever they live. He's their Master as well as ours!"

The church is people who have entered into a relationship with Jesus and therefore have been forgiven ("cleaned up") by Jesus. The church is people who understand that they want to live for Jesus ("set apart for a God-filled life"). And the church is people everywhere who call Jesus Lord of their lives.

So growing in a relationship with Jesus is helped by being *in* a church. (There's the *in* word again.) You can *go* to church, but you won't experience the church at its fullest until you "enter into" the church through relationships of commitment and service. And it's here in the church, with other believers, where we learn, grow, ask questions, serve, and seek and worship God together. In the church, brand-new Christians are together with more mature Christians and with people just getting started in seeking faith. It's like a family with parents and children. And you know what? Part of the beauty of it is that the younger ones help the more mature ones grow, and the more mature ones help the younger ones grow.

In our church, one of the most beautiful pictures of this was when a man named Pete[5] became a new Christian. Talking to me (David) one day, he asked, "Can I be involved in the children's ministry?" Thinking he meant he wanted to be a teacher (we call them shepherds) of a children's group, I told him that the best way to start would be to work alongside an experienced shepherd so he could learn. "That's not what I'm asking about," he said. "I'm wondering if

....

5   This is the other angle on Pete's story. Pete shared in his own
     words in the beginning of chapter 1.

I can be *in* the children's ministry—because I don't know anything about the Bible, and I figure that's the best place to learn it."

Stunned by the beauty of Pete's humility, I said, "You mean you want to be in a kids' group?"

"Well, yes," he replied.

I said, "Yes, I think we can arrange that." It got me choked up then, and it still does today. Pete, for the next several months, was the oldest kid in his shepherd group of eight-year-old children. It's something I'll never forget—he "became like a child" as he was entering the kingdom of God (Matthew 18:4; Mark 10:15).

When we talk about being in church, we're aware that some people may say, "I don't have to go to church to be a Christian." That's true; you don't actually have to. But you won't grow to the maturity that God has in mind if you don't enter into a church. And yes, you do need to ask yourself if that attitude is arrogance—if you are thinking, *I'm better than those people.* If you're thinking that, you've got growing to do. Maybe you are thinking, *Well, I've been hurt by the church.* What you mean is, *I've been hurt by people in a church.* True, that happens. Because a church isn't a building or a perfect institution. It's people. So people hurt people, and things go wrong. But the church is still unique and set apart by God. One of the analogies God used to describe the church (i.e., the people who are *in* Christ) is as a bride. If you think about a bride for a moment, you'll probably come up with some great descriptor words: *beautiful, special, cherished, adorned.* This is the way God thinks about His people, the church. So it makes sense that God is fully committed to the church and cares deeply about the role of the church today.

Hopefully you may consider finding a church, even if you've been hurt before or even if you've thought it didn't matter before. So what should you look for in a church? Let's make it simple. At the top you want faithfulness to the Bible, leadership with integrity, and an environment of authenticity. Faithfulness to the Bible means that the teaching you hear comes from the Bible. It isn't just feel-good analogies or stories; it's actually truth being told from what the Bible says. Leadership with integrity is sometimes harder to discern immediately, but you are looking for men and women who lead the church with humility, honesty, and transparency. This kind of leadership usually cultivates a spirit of authenticity in the community. One of our favorite church "taglines" is this: "A place where everyone is welcome, no one is perfect, and anything is possible!"[6] That kind of environment says, "Hey, come on in no matter where you are with God; no one here is perfect, and we trust God can do great things in us, even though we're far from doing it just right." That's a great place to start with a church. After those factors, you'll be looking for a place where worship is central to life together, where there is intentional focus on growing in Christ, and where there is always a sense of reaching others so they can come into God's family.

IN GOD'S GUIDANCE: THE BIBLE

I (Nicole) was once teaching at a retreat and had a young woman approach me with some questions about God. We spoke together for several minutes about her struggles to understand who Jesus is and what He does. My very first thought at the time was, *I wish we were finished writing this book so I could give it to her!* After asking a few more questions, I recommended several books, writing them all down for her. We prayed together, and just before she walked away,

....

6   From Cross Point Church in Nashville, Tennessee.

a thought came to me. "Hey, wait, Dana[7]—one more question … have you read the Bible?"

She looked at me a little sheepishly. "No."

I took back the paper I had just handed her, scratched out every book recommendation, and wrote: "Matthew. Mark. Luke. John." (These four books are known as "the Gospels," which are narratives about Jesus. They are the first four books in the New Testament.) I told her, "Dana, if you want to understand Jesus and know God, you have to start with what God left for us to know. Start with the Bible."

The Bible tells the story of God and human beings and of God's desire to be in relationship with us. Perhaps you haven't read it, or you've found it complicated and confusing in some places. Don't let that worry you or stop you from reading. Here are the basics: the Bible is a big story about a big God and about how He is working to draw people into a personal relationship with Him. Reading the Bible is how we open ourselves to learn from God, to learn about God, and to learn about His desire and design for life. The Bible is not just one story; it is a compilation of writings inspired by God's Spirit and consisting

....

7   Dana's story, in her own words, kicks off chapter 4.

of sixty-six different books and letters. Thirty-nine books make up the Old Testament—the writing that preceded the birth of Jesus Christ—and twenty-seven books make up the New Testament—the books written after the birth of Jesus.

The Bible is a remarkable book written over a period of approximately 1,500 years. The consistency of its message, though composed over many centuries by many different men, is a testimony to the fact that the Holy Spirit inspired the writing. One way of saying this is that the Bible wasn't all written by the same man, but it was all inspired by the same mind. That mind is God the Holy Spirit.

As you grow in your relationship with Jesus Christ, you will begin to learn more about the Bible. Indeed, it is not possible to become a mature Christian without a growing knowledge of the Bible. The Bible is God's Word, and it's one of the most important ways that He has revealed Himself to us. The more you know the Bible, the more you will get to know God Himself.

STUDYING THE BIBLE

Perhaps in time you will decide to enter a Bible study with others. Bible studies can be great places to learn.

Studying the Bible and learning about the contexts in which it was written, the historical backgrounds and cultures and authors who produced it, are all important things to know as you seek to grow in your understanding of the Bible. The Bible will teach you more about yourself, about life, about God, and about other people. And as you learn and grow in your knowledge of the Bible, remember that it's about loving God with all your heart, soul, mind, and strength. It's easy over time for some people to begin to "know the Bible by head," but the Bible is intended to be known also by heart. It speaks to head and heart, to our souls and our wills.

Mostly we would encourage you to read the Bible "as a whole," learning how it is written all together. It might sound silly, but one of the best things you can do with the Bible is just read it. Read it like you read other books. Doing this helps us see the big picture of the Bible in ways that can be missed if we study it only by breaking it down into a million parts. Some people get caught up in studying the Bible by chopping it into pieces. Especially when you are just beginning, examining the Bible in so many parts is a little like trying to identify a species of fish by examining fish sticks from the grocery store. The "part" barely resembles the whole! So when you are getting started, whether you are reading or studying the Bible, remember the whole and try not to get bogged down with a million little parts. Friends don't let friends treat the Bible like a fish stick.

IN CONVERSATION WITH GOD: PRAYER

Prayer is intentional conversation with God. The purpose of prayer is the same as the purpose of other intentional conversations: to grow closer together in a meaningful relationship. This means prayer covers a wide number of topics. Prayer involves sharing ideas, listening, asking questions, asking for help, expressing so you can be understood, confessing and saying you are sorry, saying thank you, or just being together. The Bible encourages us to "pray without ceasing" (1 Thessalonians 5:17 ESV). Philippians 4:6 says, "In every situation, by prayer and petition, with thanksgiving, present your requests to God." This is a life of continual conversation with God.

I (Nicole) once heard a speaker at a middle school camp challenge the kids to say, "Dear God," before they let their feet touch the ground in the morning, and to say, "Amen," as they lie down to sleep for the night. I found that helpful because it opens our hearts and minds to the reality of God's presence and nearness in our daily lives. This is the heart of conversational prayer with God.

Prayer may also be specifically set apart in uninterrupted space because you want to have quality time with God. This is akin to any great relationship where there will be much talking throughout the day as well as those special times where you can go deeper and share in more meaningful ways. As your relationship with God grows, you'll find that you develop your own patterns and rhythms of prayer. You may pray out loud; you may pray silently; you might write or journal your prayers. You may do all of these.

In time you may pray with articulated words, or you may pray with ideas or emotions or desires that you intentionally direct to God. It's been said that prayers, one way or another, fall into just three categories: "Thank You," "Please," and "Help." We'd like to add a fourth: prayers that are not for such specific reasons, but for conversation or stillness where you simply wish to be with God. Relationships do not consist of merely words, but of time spent together, even if that time is in silence. Dallas Willard alluded to this when he described prayer as "a matter of the innermost heart's being totally open and honest before God."[8] And you know you are beginning to grow in prayer when you find yourself praying not because you want to ask God for things but solely because you want to be with Him.

To be meaningful, prayer should be intentional and authentic. There are two ways prayer can go in the wrong direction: disconnected prayers, where there is no intentionality behind what you are saying, and inauthentic prayers, where you pray for show (for yourself or others), but not with honesty of heart.

DISCONNECTED PRAYERS

Disconnected prayers are words coming out of your mouth with no express intent or heart behind them. The words become rote recitation. You may be familiar with the Lord's Prayer, which comes straight from Jesus, who taught it to His disciples; it begins, "Our Father which art in heaven" (Luke 11:1–4 KJV; Matthew 6:9–13 KJV). Perhaps you know this prayer and you've said this prayer, but it's been just that: words so familiar that they lose their meaning. Another example is what is sometimes called "saying

----

8   Dallas Willard, *The Divine Conspiracy: Rediscovering Our Hidden Life in God* (New York: HarperCollins, 1998), 195.

grace" or "a blessing" before a meal. Some people remember a prayer from childhood that their family repeated before eating. These kinds of prayers become such a rote practice that the words can be meaningless. Do you remember anything like that? "Bless this food to our use and us to Thy service, for Christ's sake. Amen." Or, "God is good; God is great; thank You for this food. Amen."

If "just saying words" was praying, then we could teach a parrot to pray, and it could be the most spiritual member of the family. But God isn't interested in rote rituals or empty words coming out of our mouths. He cares about our hearts. In 1 Samuel 16:7, the Bible says, "The LORD does not look at the things people look at. People look at the outward appearance, but the LORD looks at the heart." What this means is that a pastor of forty years could know a million different ways to pray, and it might mean nothing if his prayers don't have heart. You might be inexperienced with prayer and feel that you have no ways to pray except to say, "Wow," "Thanks," and "Help."[9] If these words are authentic, God regards them and receives them as worship. People look at outward appearances,

....

9   Anne Lamott wrote a book under the same name: *Help, Thanks, Wow: The Three Essential Prayers* (New York: Riverhead, 2012).

but God looks at the heart. That certainly evens the playing field. It's not about works and fancy words. It's about your heart.

INAUTHENTIC PRAYERS

Inauthentic prayers are prayers for show. This is when you pray for "how it will sound to other people." This is one part of what we would call the religion show, the temptation to turn your religion into a show for other people to see. So, if you are just trying to make your prayer sound good, forget it. Skip it and wait till you're ready to just be yourself. Or if you're trying to say something to another person by disguising it with prayer, this is manipulation. It's praying horizontally for someone around you instead of lifting your prayer to God and praying vertically. For instance, let's say a husband and wife are at a couples' Bible study, and at the end, in an open time of prayer, the woman starts praying, "Lord, I pray for my husband, David, that he will stop leaving his socks on the floor and that he will stop leaving the cap off the toothpaste. Lord, I just pray You'll speak to him about this." Um, that's not prayer. That's spiritual manipulation. Or maybe you are at a women's Bible study and someone begins praying for her mother-in-law: "Lord, I just hope

You'll change John's mom. Make her stop being so controlling and overbearing in our lives. Help her to know that her new relationship with the guy she's dating doesn't honor You. Protect me and my children from her terrible ways." Well, that's not prayer either. That's gossip.

Dale Bruner wrote, "Prayer must be vertical to be honest. Directing an activity that is supposed to be directed to God into an activity that can also make a good impression on others—Jesus calls phony."[10]

Sometimes the most meaningful praying is full of stops and starts, "ahs" and "ums." The best praying is praying like a child—honest, earnest, unpretentious. Pray like that. Often.

IN TAKING ACTION: SERVING

Authentic Christianity will show forth in a love and care for God and people. Jesus described the sum of all the law and commandments as, "'And you shall love the Lord your God with all your heart and with all your soul and with all your mind and with all your strength.' The second is this: 'You shall love your neighbor as yourself'" (Mark 12:30–31 ESV). The beauty of this statement is

....

10   Frederick Dale Bruner, *The Christbook: Matthew 1–12: A Commentary, Volume 1* (Dallas: Word Publishing, 1987), 234.

that love for both God and people is present if a person's relationship with God is real. To serve people but have no love for God is not God-centered love and service. To love God but do and care nothing for those around you suggests that the love for God either is not real or is significantly lacking. You see, God loves people—so if you love God and are truly growing in your relationship with God, you will also be growing in a love for people.

Taking action by serving, by caring, by stepping outward toward people is expressing the heart of God's love to people, and it is also a significant way that you will grow in your own relationship with Jesus. Why? Because this is what Jesus did. He gave Himself for others. As you do this, He will be with you and you will grow in Him. This can be as simple as offering a listening ear to a person who is going through a hard time, or it may be more extensive than that. It is *offering yourself* one way or another. It could be your time, your help, your money, your love, your presence. But what's clear is that you take action and you serve. Jesus said, "For even the Son of Man did not come to be served, but to serve" (Mark 10:45).

Like prayer, serving should be authentic and not for show. If you are doing good so others will think, *What a great guy!* you might want to skip this as well. If you're doing it so the person you are serving will thank you profusely or "owe you one," you might be serving, but it's not in the name of Jesus.

A simple way to grow in serving God and others is to start the day by asking God to give you eyes to see the needs around you. This made all the difference for our friend Craig, who said, "It takes thought and energy to put yourself in a position to really make a difference. Now that God is in my life, I'm able to see and have the energy to move on opportunities much more than I used to. He's given me eyes to see that. I look at life through a different window now. The perspective is much different. It was like the shades were drawn, and now they are up."

IN THE ACT OF PRAISE: WORSHIP

When I (David) first heard the idea of a person "praising God," it threw me off. I envisioned a parent saying to a child, "Good boy, Billy—you did so well." The interaction sounded like one where we'd kind of give a pat on the head. I didn't think God needed or wanted a pat on the head from me. While I now know that it's true—He doesn't need a pat on the head from me—I was missing the point. To praise is to express appreciation for or to someone. Worship is our intentional expression of appreciation and gratitude and wonder to God.

Worship can be done alone or in a stadium with thousands of others. It can take place in a church building or in a mountain meadow. Worship can be beautiful in solitude, and it can be thrilling in the company of many others who share this same heart toward God and are pouring out their hearts to Him together.

Worship is your authentic and honest expression toward God. Worship services may be done with choirs or electric guitars, in formal or informal clothes. None of that is what really matters. What matters is that it's authentic and honest—never a show—and that our hearts are really in it. In the New Testament Jesus said, "True worshipers will worship the Father in the Spirit and in truth, for they are the kind of worshipers the Father seeks" (John 4:23). In the Old Testament, God spoke against worshipping for show when He said things like, "These people … honor me with their lips, but their hearts are far from me" (Isaiah 29:13), or, "I hate your religious feasts; what I desire is a contrite heart" (see Amos 5; Psalm 51).

Sometimes you might hear people come out of a worship service saying to each other, "How did you like the worship?" This leads to an analysis of the songs (good or bad), a critique of the choir or worship leader, etc., all of which is beside the point. The heart of the matter is not "How did you like the worship?" but "How did God like *your* worship?"

You may find worship a little awkward at first, as you go from just singing words or listening to words to really taking them in and then expressing them with your heart. You might find yourself thinking, *I'm not sure if I believe that,* or *That's not true for me right now.* That's actually a step in the right direction, because you are interacting with the words and experiencing them for what they are meant to be—an honest inter-action and expression toward God. So keep at it. Keep thinking about the words, and even when your heart doesn't feel "in it," keep listening; keep singing; keep interacting. Many worship songs are straight from Scripture, so as you listen to them and learn them, you are getting to know who God is, and that will help you know Him in a deeper way.

Our friend Hunter, whose story began this chap-ter, said it this way: "I think some people measure how much they love God by how loudly they can sing, how high their hands are raised, and how well they can harmonize with the worship leader. But God has taught me that worship is a chance to give back my gratitude."

Next is the matter of freshness in worship—because if love is real, it is creative. Interestingly, the Bible says, "Sing to the LORD a new song; sing to the LORD, all the earth" (Psalm 96:1). The emphasis is on the "new" song, a fresh expression of devotion.

Look at it this way: let's say that every time Elisabeth has a birthday, I (David) get her the same card (the very same one) and the same half-dozen roses from the same discount flower shop. Well, the first time or two, it might be okay, but after a number of times the gesture begins to feel empty, kind of hollow in its same-ness. She might think, *Um, thanks, kinda, I think. Same old, same old.* If my love for her is authentic, I want to let her know in new ways how I appreciate her. Amazingly, with our loving, relational God, it's the same way. True love is creative.

Finally, worship not only expresses our growing love for God but also actually *increases* our love for God as we experience His presence and let Him shape our hearts. This is partly because God is present when His people are gathered. Matthew 18:20 records Jesus saying, "Where two or three gather in my name, there am I with them." This suggests there is a power and joy when believers are gathered that doesn't happen when we're not together. Makes worshipping God sound kind of like spending time with a loving Father who loves to be with all His children. Sounds like a really awesome party!

So now we've talked about "how do I grow from here?" To summarize, this happens as we root deeply (abide) into Jesus, giving our lives to Him and allowing Him to give His life to us.

- *In* Relationships: the Church
- *In* God's Guidance: the Bible
- *In* Conversation with God: Prayer
- *In* Taking Action: Serving
- *In* the Act of Praise: Worship

A FINAL WORD

Like we said at the outset, your journey doesn't end here—it begins. In some ways, we think of this entire book as a preamble or a preface to your life with God. It starts here with this honest search, with some foundational truths and a few reminders. Remember that this life with Jesus is not something you accomplish or master; it's a growing relationship from this day forward.

We've concluded *Start Here* with this chapter on practical next steps for your journey. And our desire and prayer is that you would continue to seek after God—to press through the objections, to lean closer into Him in hard times, to ask your questions of God, and to seek to answer His questions for you. And we pray for you the same way the apostle Paul prayed for the early church:

> I pray that Christ will be more and more at home in your hearts as you trust in him. May your roots go down deep into the soil of God's marvelous love. And may you have the power to understand, as all God's people should, how wide, how long, how high, and how deep his love really is. (Ephesians 3:17–19 NLT)

And to this beginning, and to your next steps, we say,

Amen!

FURTHER READING

. . . .

Where do you go from here? Here's a brief list of resources for "next steps" to help you in your relationship with God.

BIBLES

You need a Bible, and the choices seem infinite. Every English Bible is a translation from the original languages (Hebrew for the Old Testament, Greek for the New). Because it's a translation, different versions or translations vary slightly from one another. Over time you may prefer one over the others. There are also Bible apps available for your phone, complete with multiple translations and reading plans, which are a great free resource. For a print version, here are a few Bibles we recommend.

The NIV Study Bible (Zondervan)

This Bible will give you historical context for each book within the Bible and extensive cross-references (which help you connect themes that occur through-out the Bible). This Bible is known for extensive, scholarly study notes at the bottom of each page as well as a concordance, which allows you to search the Bible by word.

Life Application Study Bible NLT (Tyndale)

This Bible provides less in-depth study notes but more devotional thoughts on how to make passages from the Bible personal for your life.

The Message (NavPress)

The Message is a modern rendering of the Bible written by Eugene Peterson. Rather than being translated verse by verse by a group of Bible scholars, *The Message* is one man's endeavor to present the content and heart of the Bible through a modern expression for our time. This is a great companion to a study Bible.

DEVOTIONALS

A devotional is a book designed to help you in a daily relationship with God. It's usually written in short segments, meant to be read to help you connect with God and to grow in your understanding of Him.

My Utmost for His Highest, Oswald Chambers (Discovery House)

This is one of the most-read religious books of all time. With 365 daily readings, *My Utmost for His Highest* will encourage you to think deeply about how loving God changes everything about your life. While this is an excellent devotional book, some might suggest it is harder for new believers to understand. Go to www.utmost.org to read the devotional, or download the app for your phone.

God's Best for My Life, Lloyd John Ogilvie (Harvest House Publishers)

Written by a former chaplain of the US Senate, this daily devotional helps the reader see God in every circumstance. Easy to read with a wide variety of examples.

Devotional Classics, Richard Foster and James Bryan Smith (HarperOne)

This is a collection of fifty-two devotional writers from the past and present. This book will give you great exposure to a wide range of voices while also deepening your understanding of a well-balanced spiritual life with God.

CHRISTIAN LIVING/THEOLOGY

As you continue your relationship with God, you will encounter questions about faith and life. Most likely, many of your questions are similar to those that other people have had over the centuries, and you'll want to try to understand more. These books can help.

Crazy Love, Francis Chan (David C Cook)

If *Start Here* is Christianity 1.0, *Crazy Love* is Christianity 1.1. This book will take you deeper into the character of God and the nature of your relationship with Him. If you want more after reading about the attributes of God in chapter 5, this is your next step.

Who Is This Man? The Unpredictable Impact of the Inescapable Jesus, John Ortberg (Zondervan)

An exploration into who Jesus is, what He offers, what He taught, and what He's done for us. John Ortberg is the pastor of Menlo Park Presbyterian Church in California. To listen to his sermons, visit the church's website, http://mppc.org.

Forgotten God, Francis Chan (David C Cook)

The Holy Spirit, "the shy member of the Trinity," is the most abstract and perhaps least-understood aspect of God. *Forgotten God* provides a thorough biblical study to help us know who the Holy Spirit is and how He works in our lives.

The Life You've Always Wanted, John Ortberg (Zondervan)

John Ortberg introduces us to the concept of spiritual disciplines in easy-to-understand, accessible language. Spiritual disciplines are practices and habits that we can use to open our hearts to God's voice and His work in our lives.

Mere Christianity, C. S. Lewis (HarperOne)

C. S. Lewis, who wrote the children's series The Chronicles of Narnia, might be best known for this book. *Mere Christianity* provides a reasoned argument for the existence of God. It is deep, convicting, and intellectually rigorous. If you want to go deeper into understanding the "why" behind the way of God in the world, this is a next step.

The Reason for God, Timothy Keller (Dutton)

Timothy Keller has been called the "modern-day Lewis" because of the way he reasons through faith with intelligence and heart. This book will provide understanding of the why of Jesus—of sin, sacrifice, and the cross and resurrection. Since Keller is a contemporary author, you can also go online to access his sermons from his church in New York City, Redeemer Presbyterian.

Redeeming Love, Francine Rivers (Multnomah)

You may wonder why we're recommending a Christian historical romance novel, but *Redeeming Love* manages to capture the heart of God's relentless love for us in a way that has captivated millions. A modern retelling of the biblical book of Hosea, *Redeeming Love* is set during the California gold rush and follows the story of a bitter, cynical prostitute and a faithful farmer. Many have found that this book expresses the heart of God in a way that brings them closer to Him, so it's worth checking out.